Welcome to
Utah

by **Pat Bagley**

Welcome to Utah

Printed in the United States

First Edition

9 8 7 6 5 4 3 2 1

LCCN 2001097737

ISBN 1-56684-608-0

Welcome to
Utah

by **Pat Bagley**

Acknowledgements

Thanks to Linda Bult and Marti Esplin for proofing, editing, and providing perspective and much needed common sense. To Dave Bjorkman, Kim Clark, Chris Drysdale, Kent Frogley, Brad Hardy, Joel Jensen, Mark Knudsen, Leslie Thomas, Alan Whitesides, and Scott Young for their suggestions and intelligent advice. And to my in-house *Calvin and Hobbes* scholars, Buzz and Alec, who aren't afraid to let me know when a cartoon is just plain dumb.

For Margaret

Author's Note

Visitors to Utah see our McDonalds and our Gaps and our Starbucks and think it looks just like anywhere else in America. This is a big relief to visitors. They arrive wondering if their daughters will be kidnapped into polygamy or they'll be beaten with a cane for wanting a cocktail. But they come and find they like us. They really like us! They like our clean streets and our friendly people. And that is a big relief to us as we care deeply that no one think us weird.

But deep down anyone who's spent time here knows the truth: Utahns are fiercely weird. You hold the proof in your hands. A visitor from Poughkeepsie might pick up this book, and without any outside assistance, glean the meaning from a number of the cartoons. Now watch his brow furrow at the mention of CTR rings, Mr. Mac, the Celestial Kingdom, and 3.2 beer. You have knowledge that he doesn't have access to and you scuttle away before he can ask for enlightenment.

I've attempted to neatly group the cartoons by subject: Coming to Utah, Skiing, Outdoors, Religion, Politics, and Culture. As in life, things get messy and defy neat catagorization. As a result the book is something of a mess. For instance, there's no good reason for not grouping Skiing with Outdoors, other than I took a notion not to. Sadly, it only gets worse. Utahns mix their Religion, Culture, and Politics with abandon (I was going to say "promiscuously," but that would give entirely the wrong idea) which made sorting tough. But I've tried to stick to the general idea that some things are generally cultural and others generally religious or political. You get the general idea.

I cannot easily conceive of anything more cozy than the night in Salt Lake which we spent in a Gentile den, smoking pipes and listening to the tales of how heedless people often come to Utah and make remarks about Brigham, or polygamy, or some other sacred matter, and the very next morning at daylight such parties are sure to be found lying up some back alley, contentedly waiting for the hearse.

—Mark Twain

Coming to
Utah

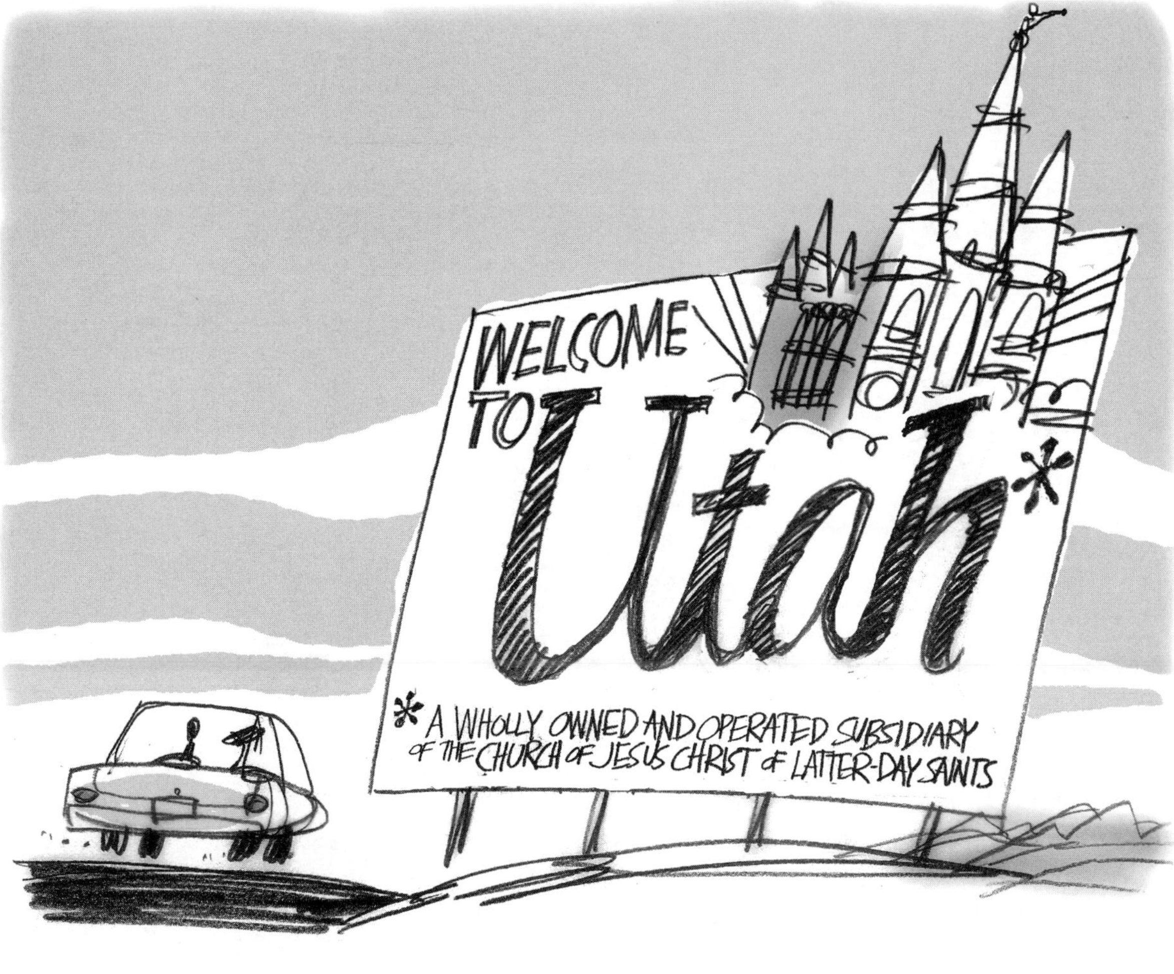
WELCOME TO Utah*
* A WHOLLY OWNED AND OPERATED SUBSIDIARY OF THE CHURCH OF JESUS CHRIST OF LATTER-DAY SAINTS

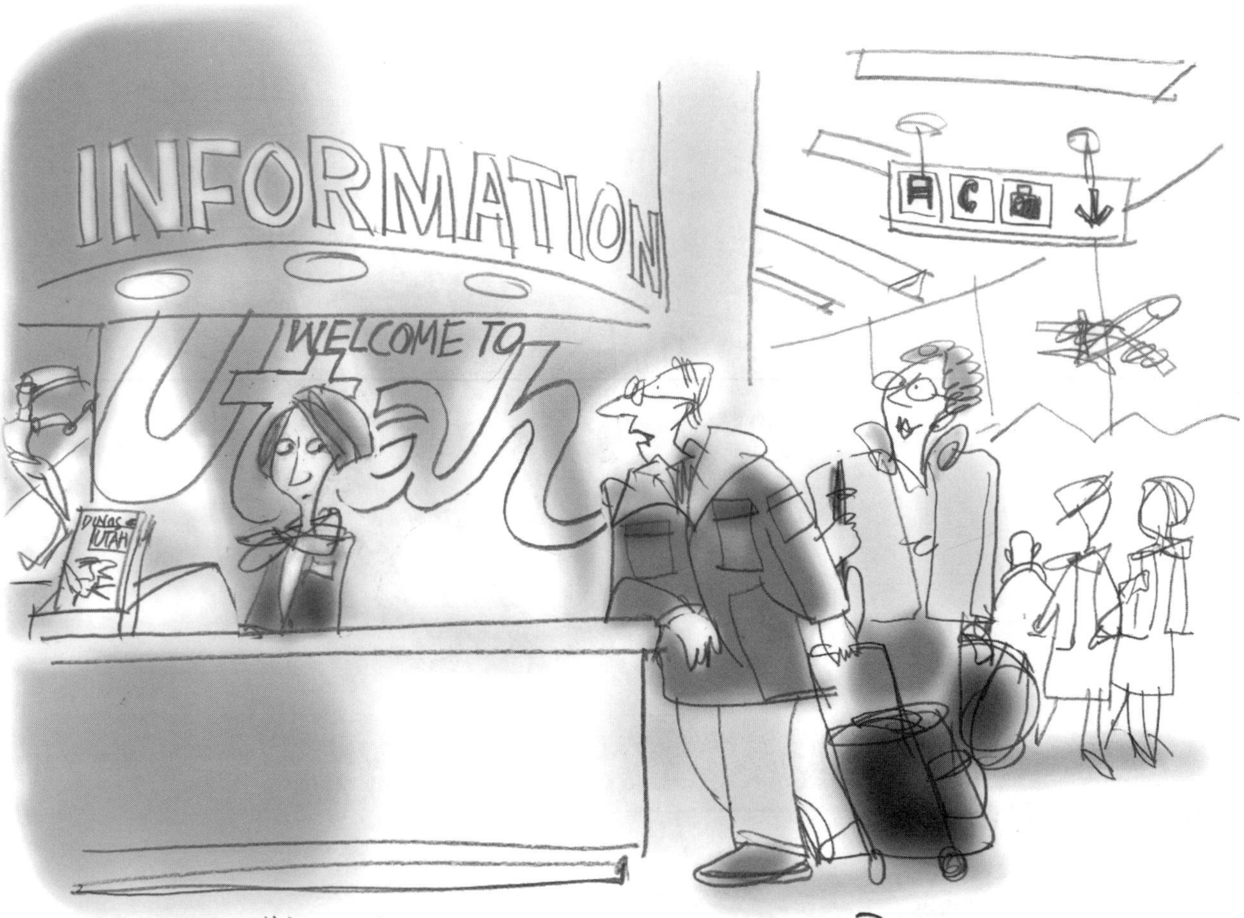
INFORMATION
WELCOME TO
Utah
DINOS of UTAH

"WHERE DO WE GET BRIBED?"

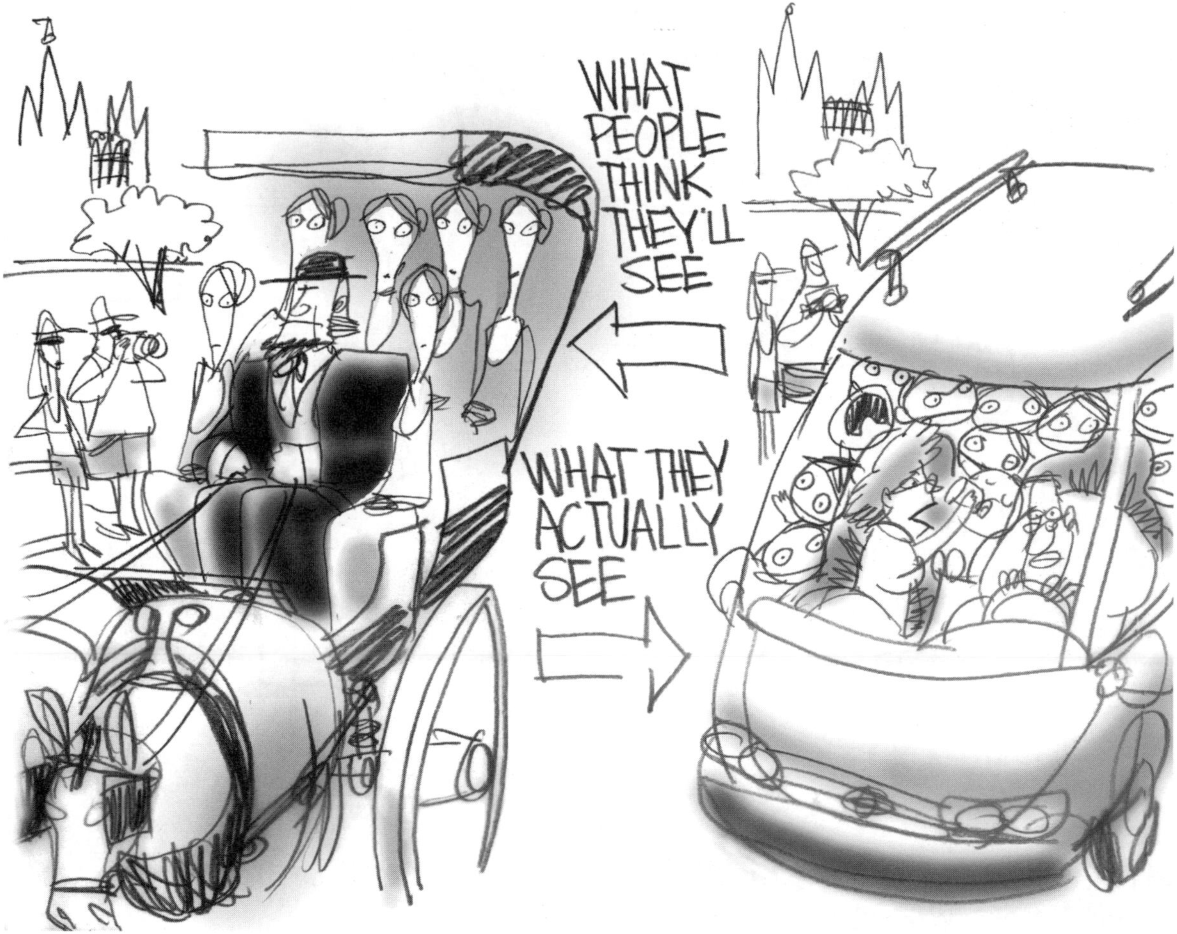
WHAT PEOPLE THINK THEY'LL SEE
WHAT THEY ACTUALLY SEE

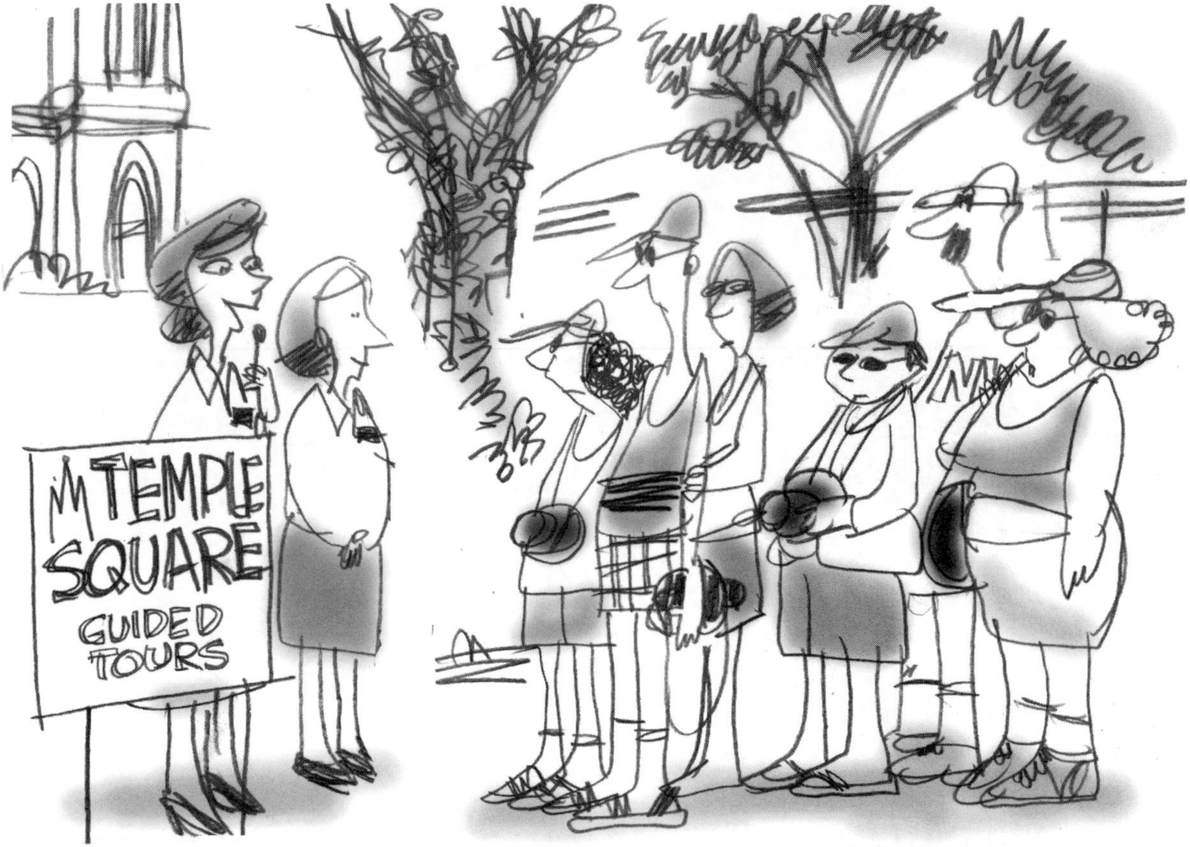
TEMPLE
SQUARE
GUIDED
TOURS

"WHY, YES, MORMONS USED TO PRACTICE POLYGAMY – PROOF OF ITS DIVINE ORIGIN IS THAT WE DIDN'T ENJOY IT FOR A SINGLE SECOND."

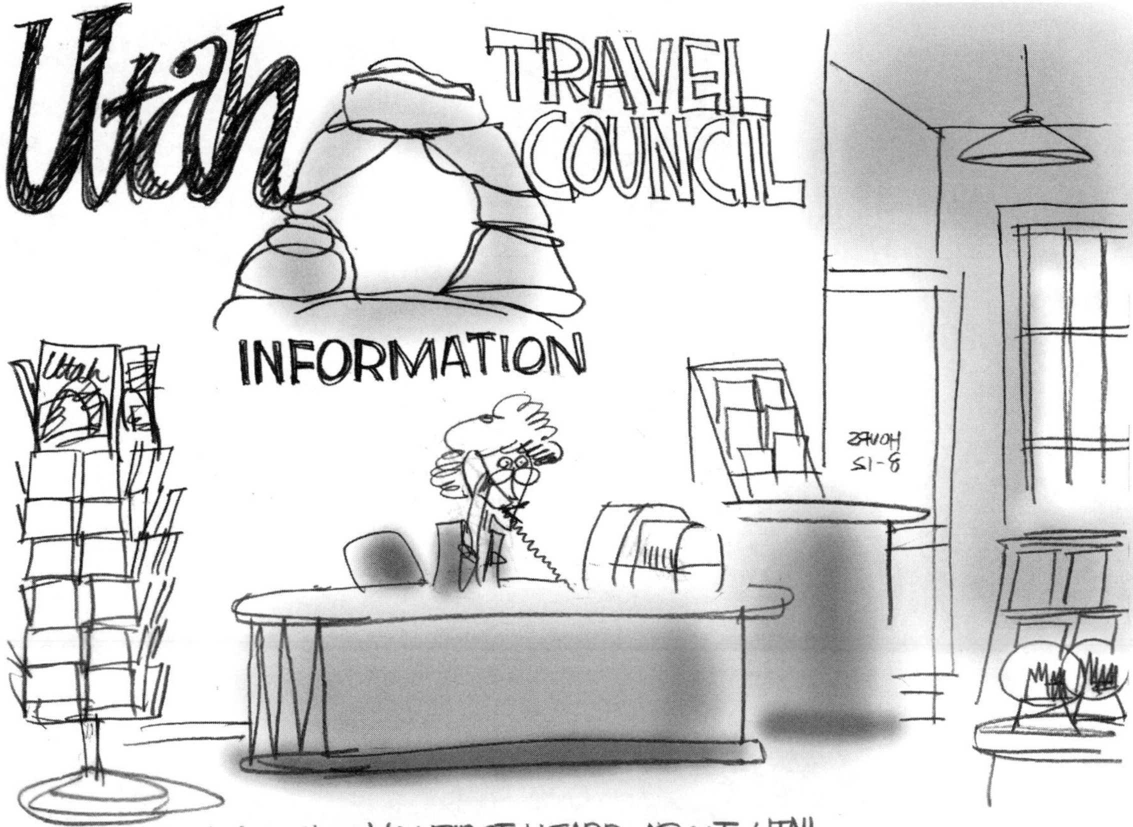
Utah
TRAVEL COUNCIL
INFORMATION
Utah

"MAY I ASK HOW YOU FIRST HEARD ABOUT UTAH — ADVERTISING SUPPLEMENT?.. WORD OF MOUTH?.. SIXTY MINUTES?"

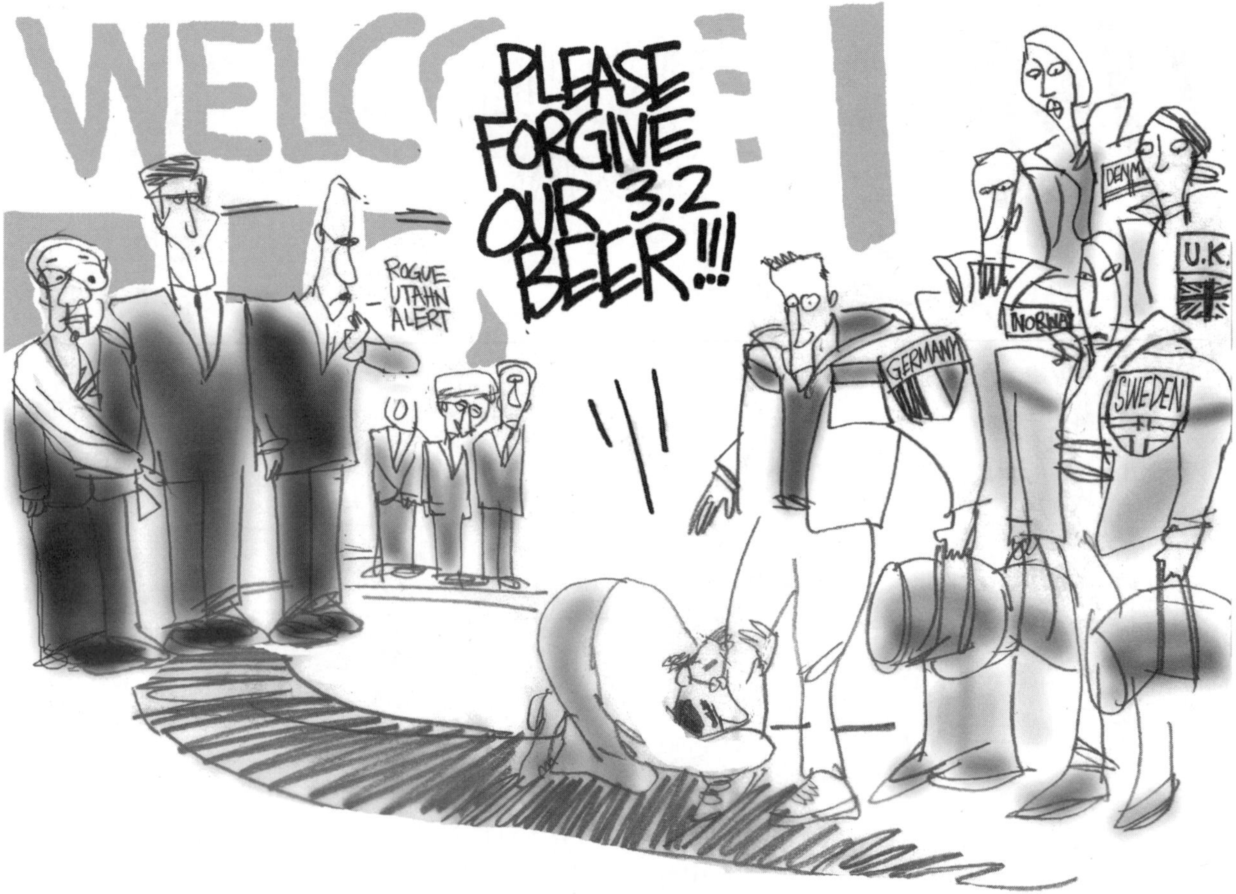
PLEASE FORGIVE OUR 3.2 BEER!!!
ROGUE UTAHN ALERT
GERMANY
NORWAY
U.K.
SWEDEN

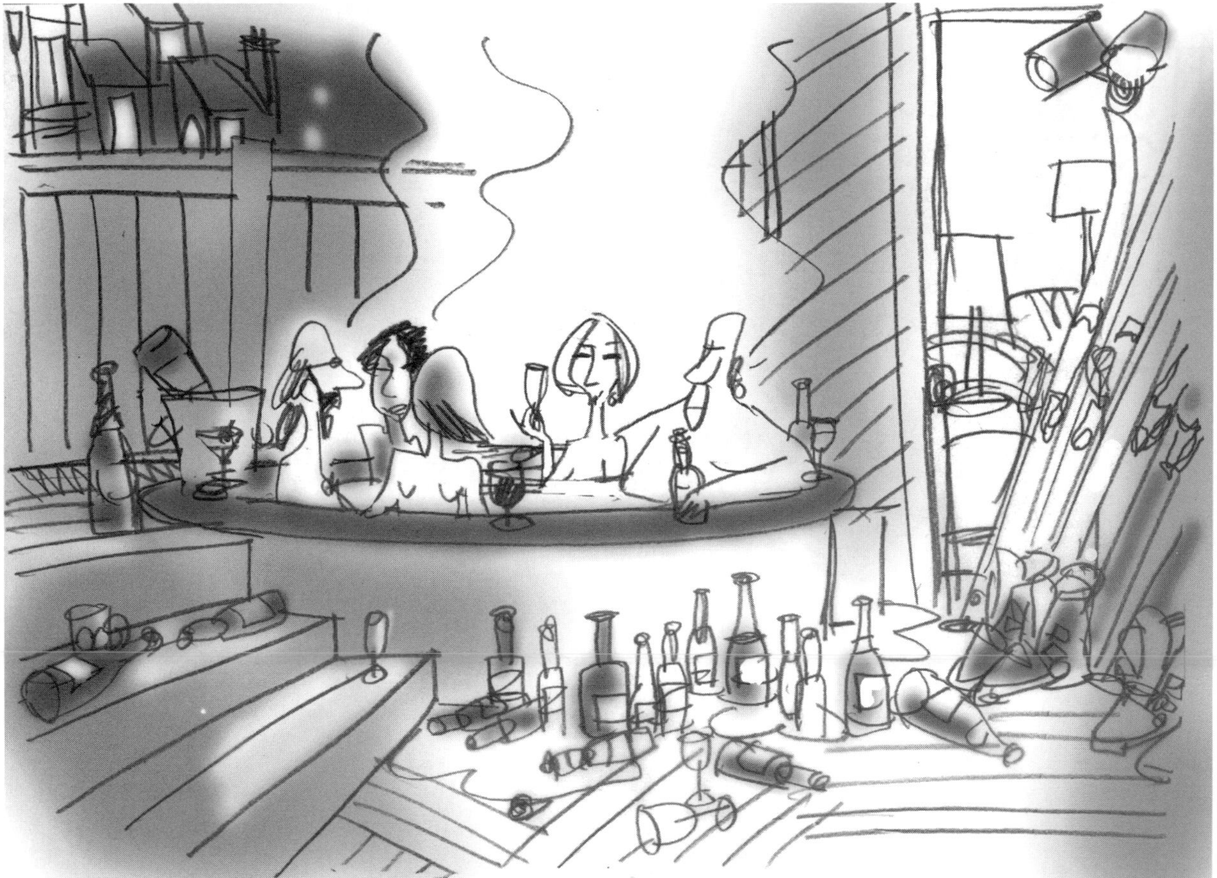

"'REPRESSIVE' DOESN'T EVEN BEGIN TO DESCRIBE THIS PLACE."

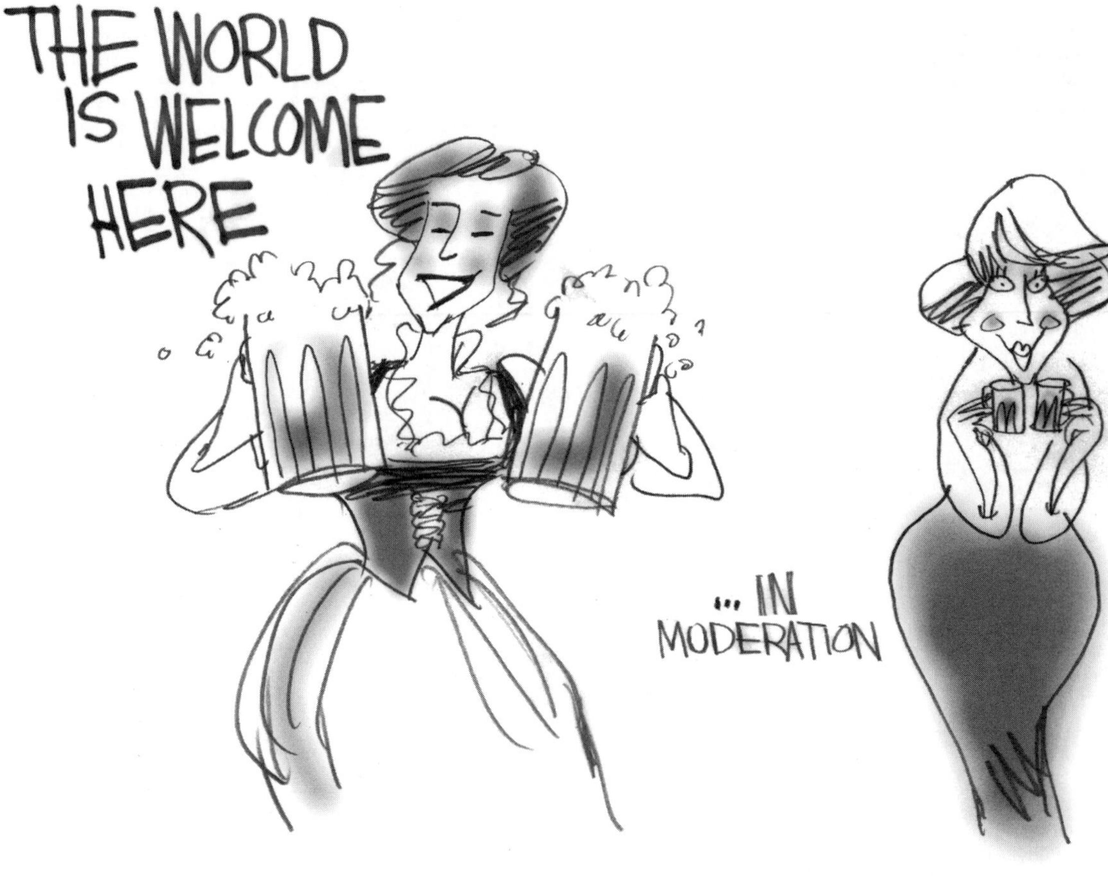
THE WORLD IS WELCOME HERE
... IN MODERATION

17

The Greatest Snow on Earth!

—Motto on Utah license plates
that the state earned the right
to use after a lengthy legal
battle with Ringling Bros. and
Barnum & Bailey Circus

Ski *Utah*

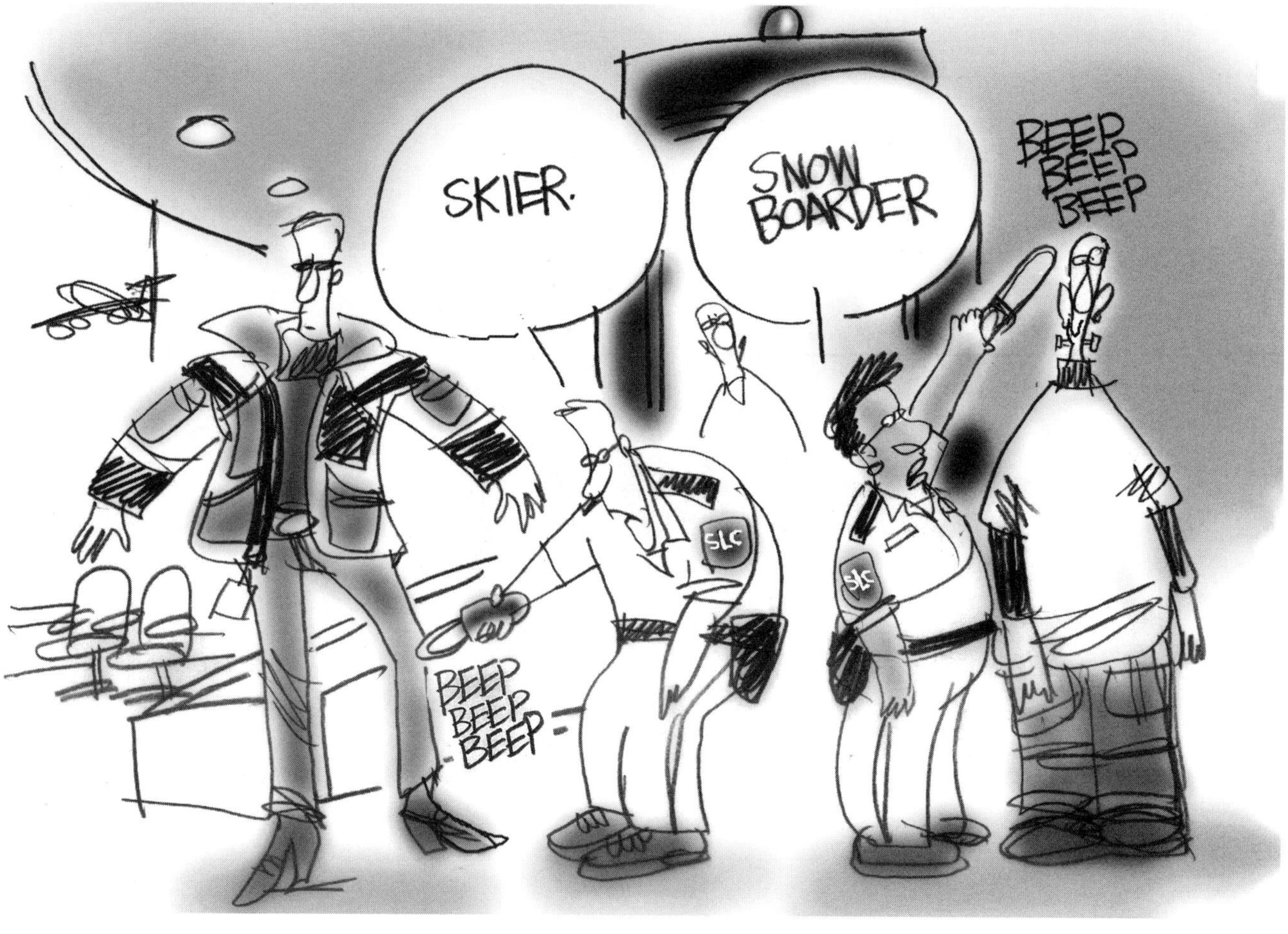
SKIER.
SNOW BOARDER
BEEP BEEP BEEP
BEEP BEEP BEEP
SLC
SLC

"THAT WAS COOL. DO IT AGAIN."

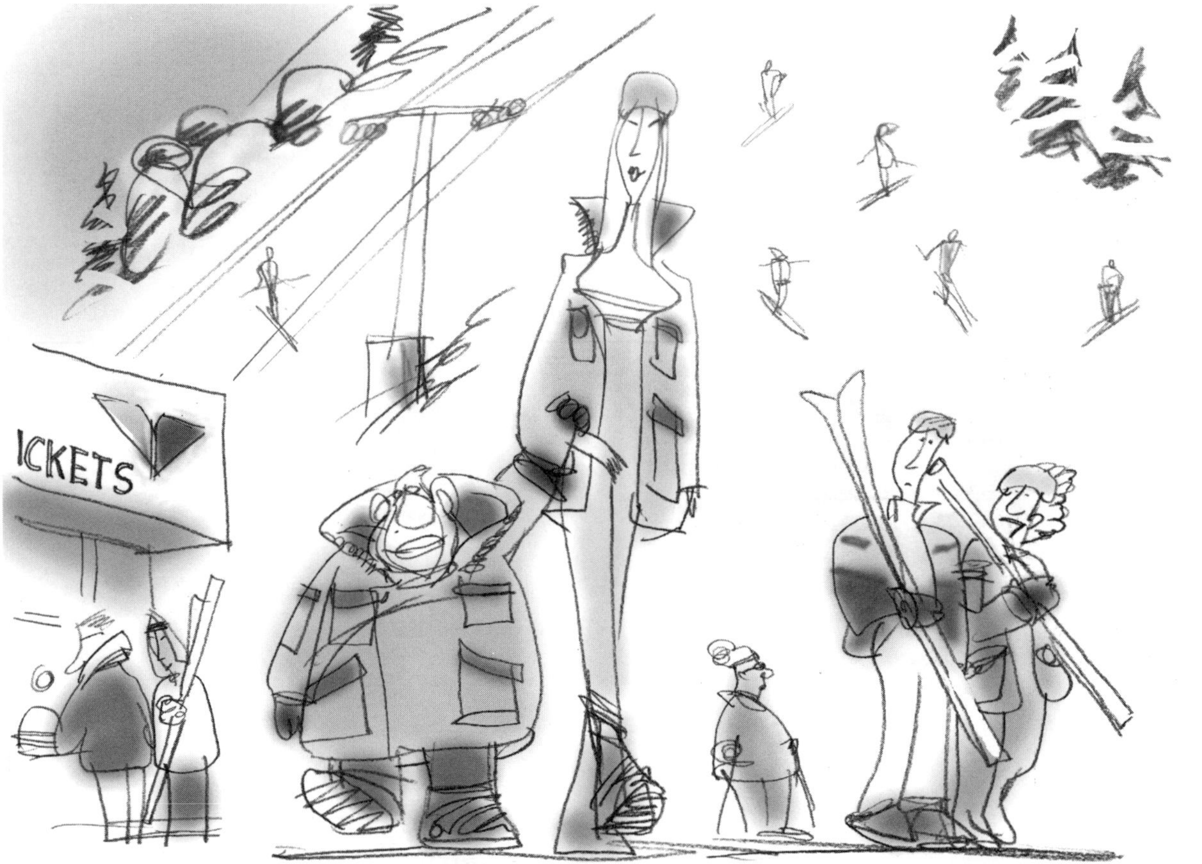
ICKETS

"THEY'VE BEEN INSEPARABLE SINCE THEY MET ON THE LIFT- AND SHE FOUND OUT HE'S WORTH FORTY MILLION."

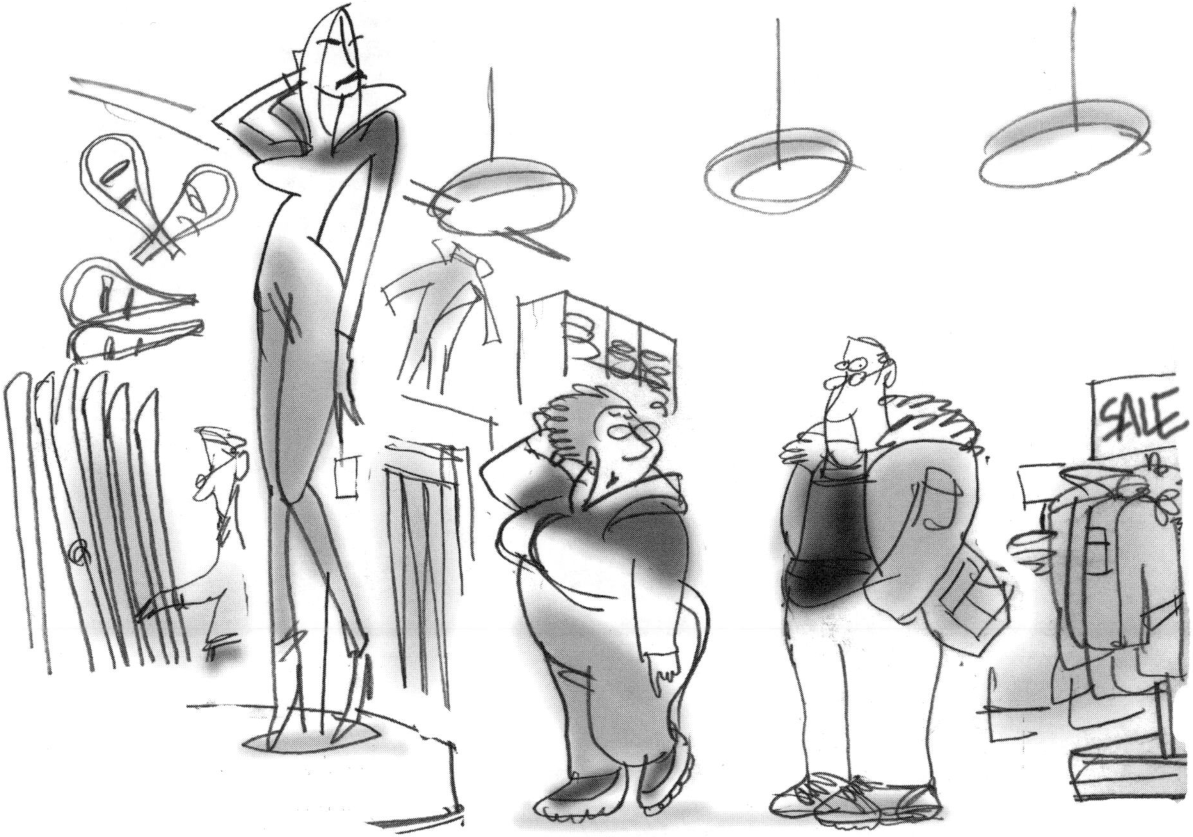
SALE

"WHAT DO YOU THINK?"

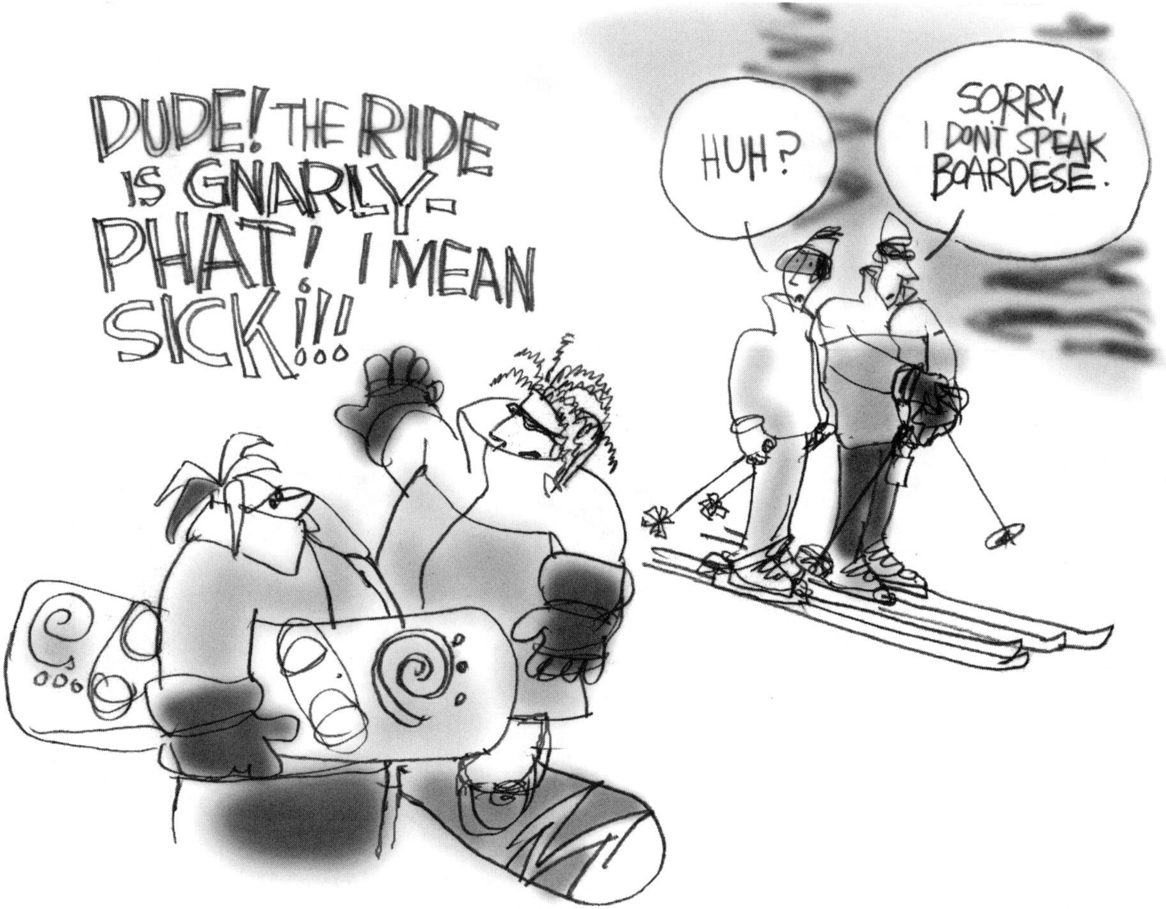
DUDE! THE RIDE IS GNARLY- PHAT! I MEAN SICK!!!
HUH?
SORRY, I DON'T SPEAK BOARDESE.

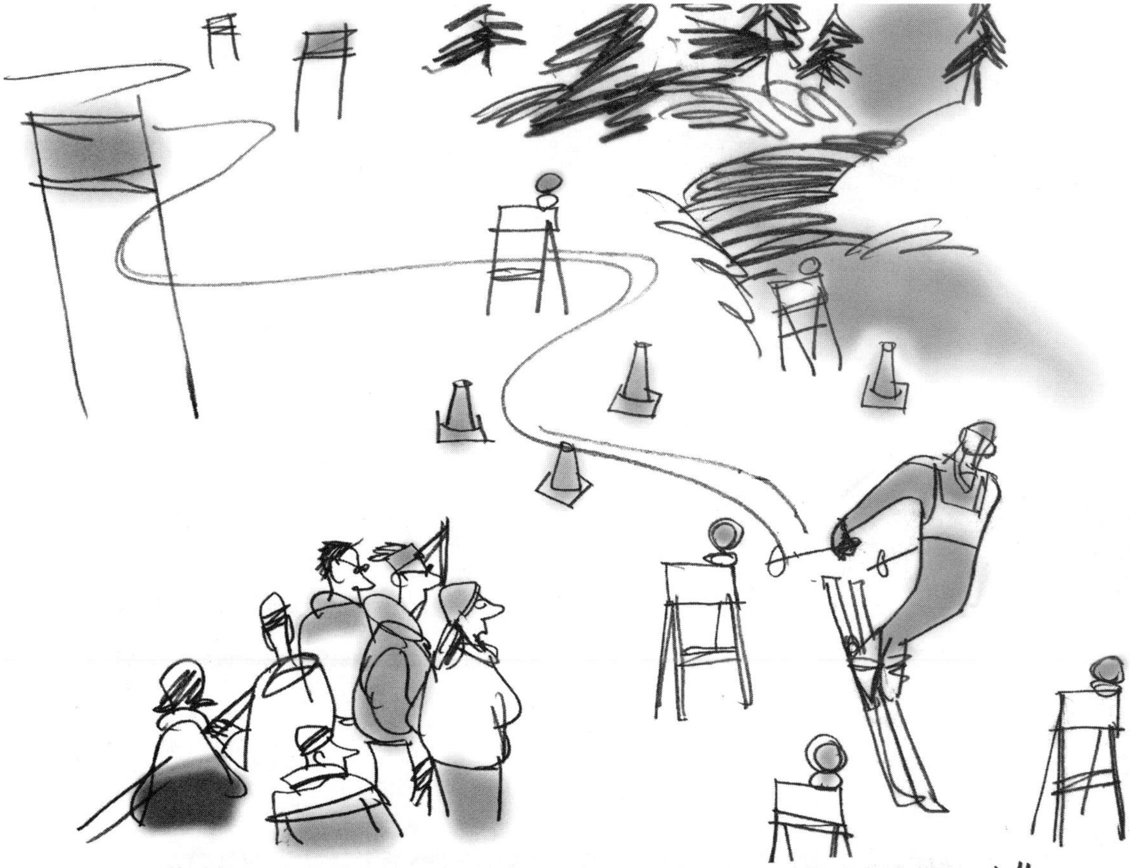

"OH, NO – HE'S GONE OFF INTO OUR ROAD CONSTRUCTION!"

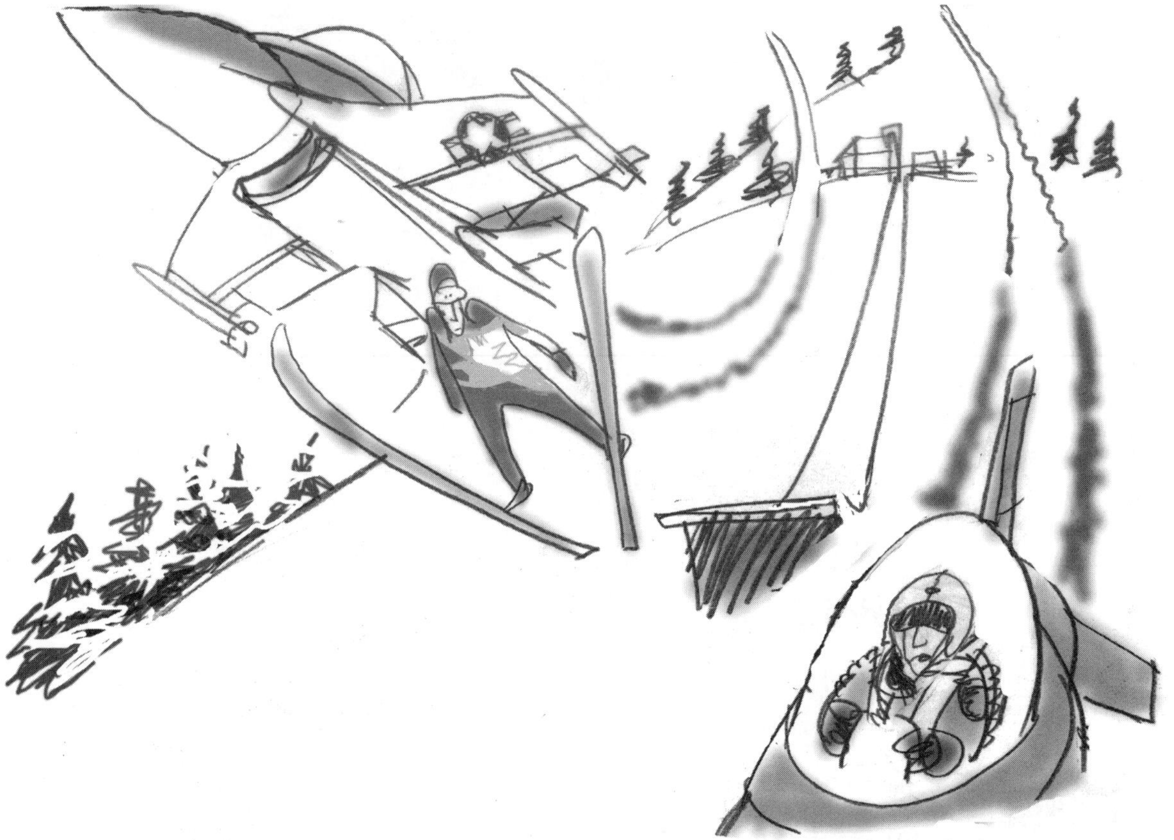

"ROGER, BASE—WE ARE ESCORTING BABY BIRD FROM THE NEST."

Utah airspace is patrolled out of security concerns for athletes.

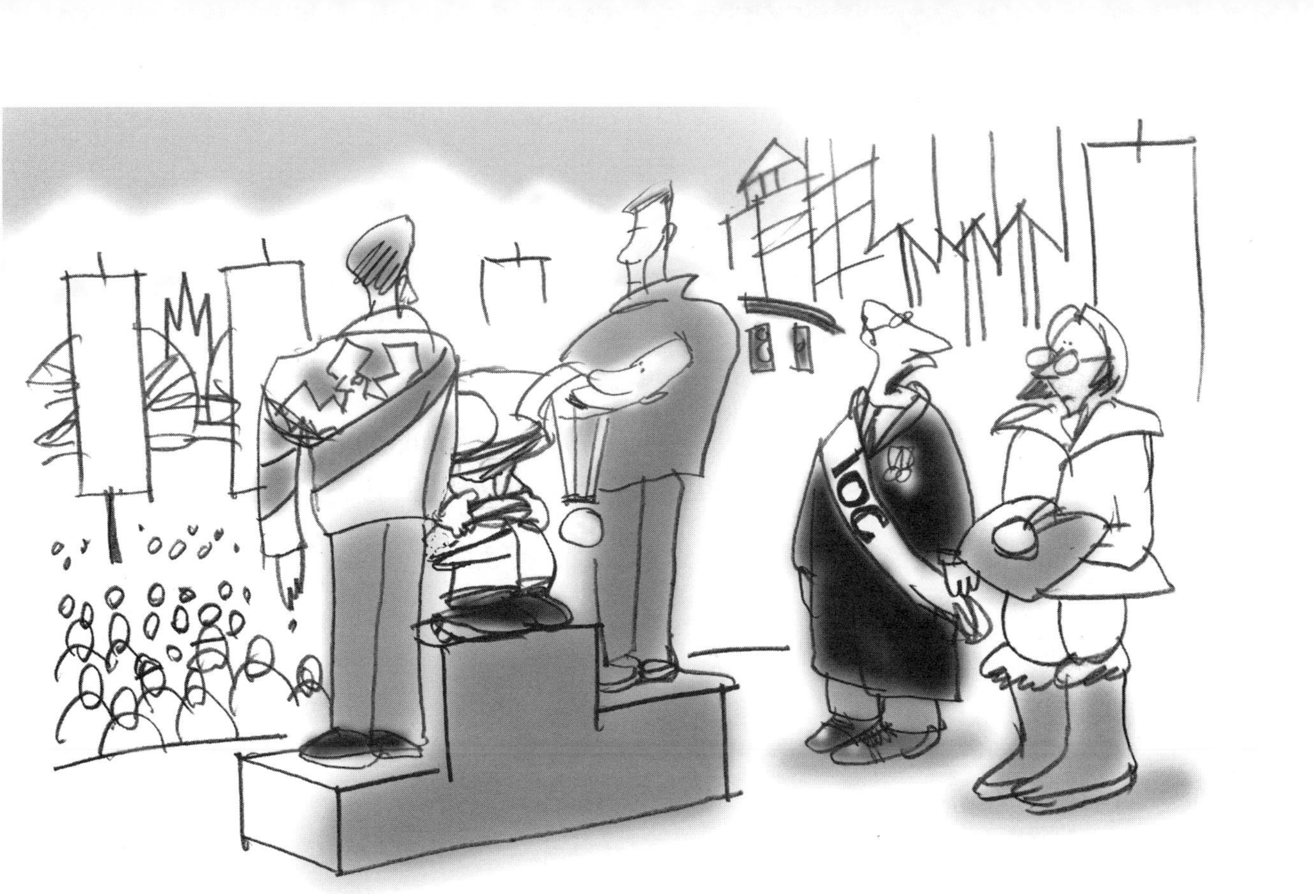
IOC

"I HAVEN'T BEEN THIS EMBARRASSED IN, OH, IT'S GOT TO BE AT LEAST A WEEK."

U.S. athletes given primer on proper etiquette at medals ceremonies.

May your trails be crooked, winding, lonesome,
dangerous, leading to the most amazing view.

—Edward Abbey

Outdoor *Utah*

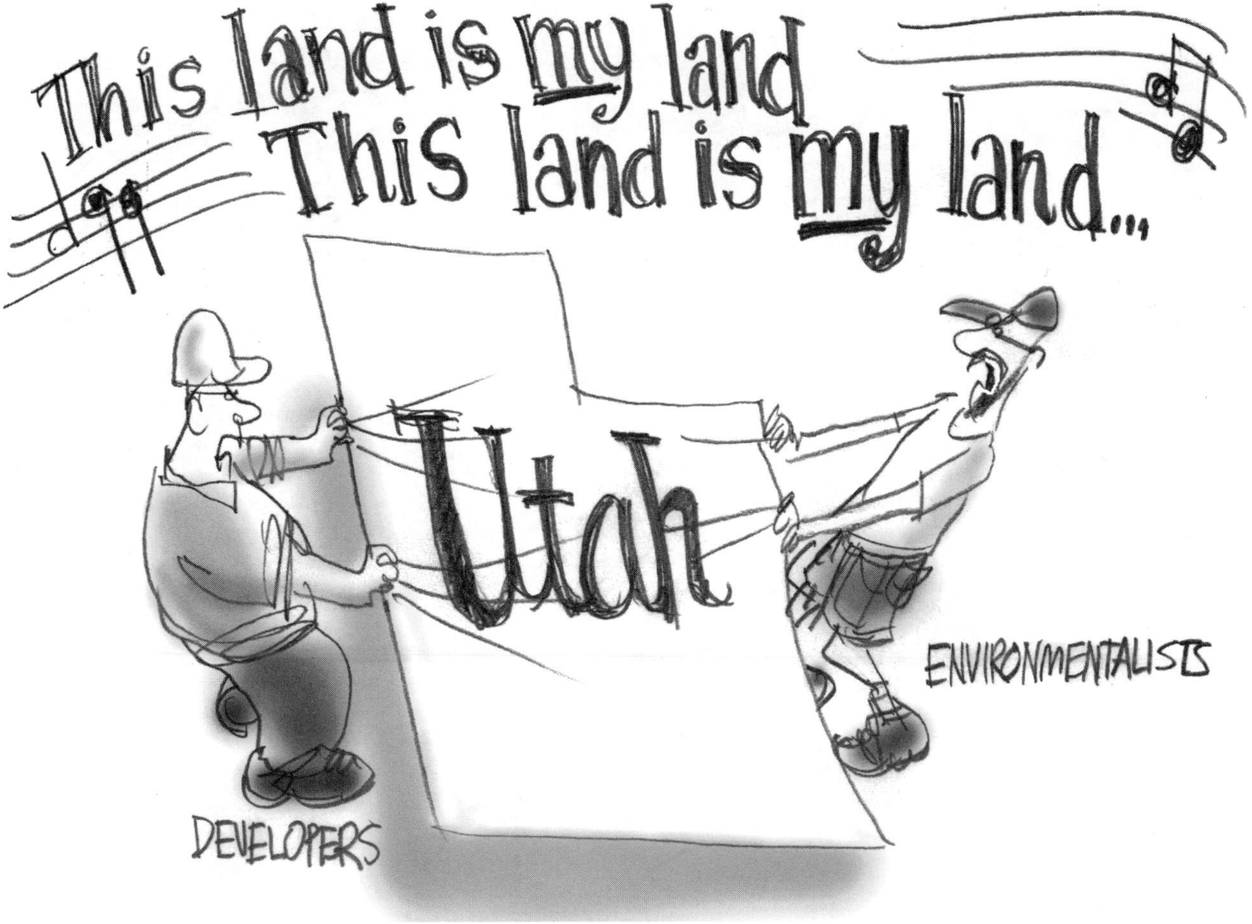
This land is my land
This land is my land...
Utah
DEVELOPERS
ENVIRONMENTALISTS

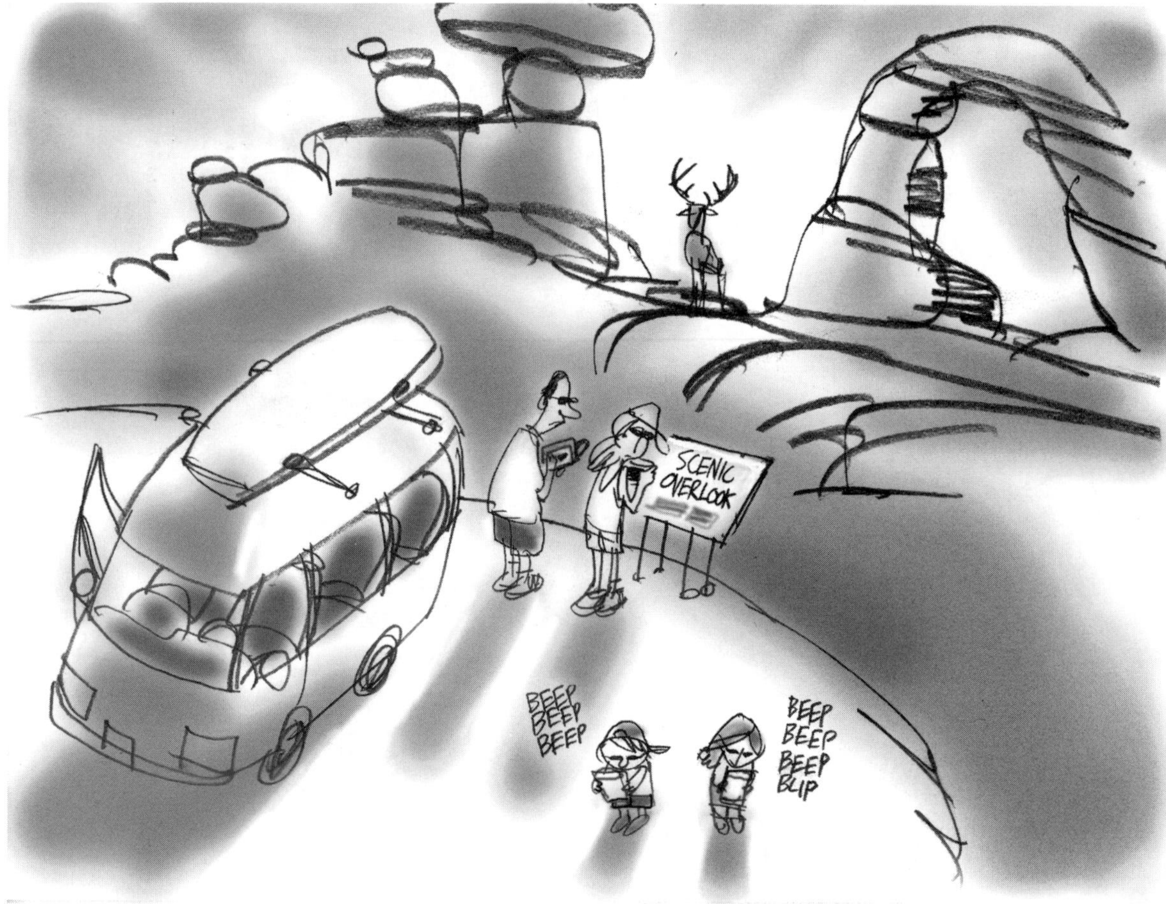
SCENIC
OVERLOOK
BEEP
BEEP
BEEP
BEEP
BEEP
BEEP
BLIP

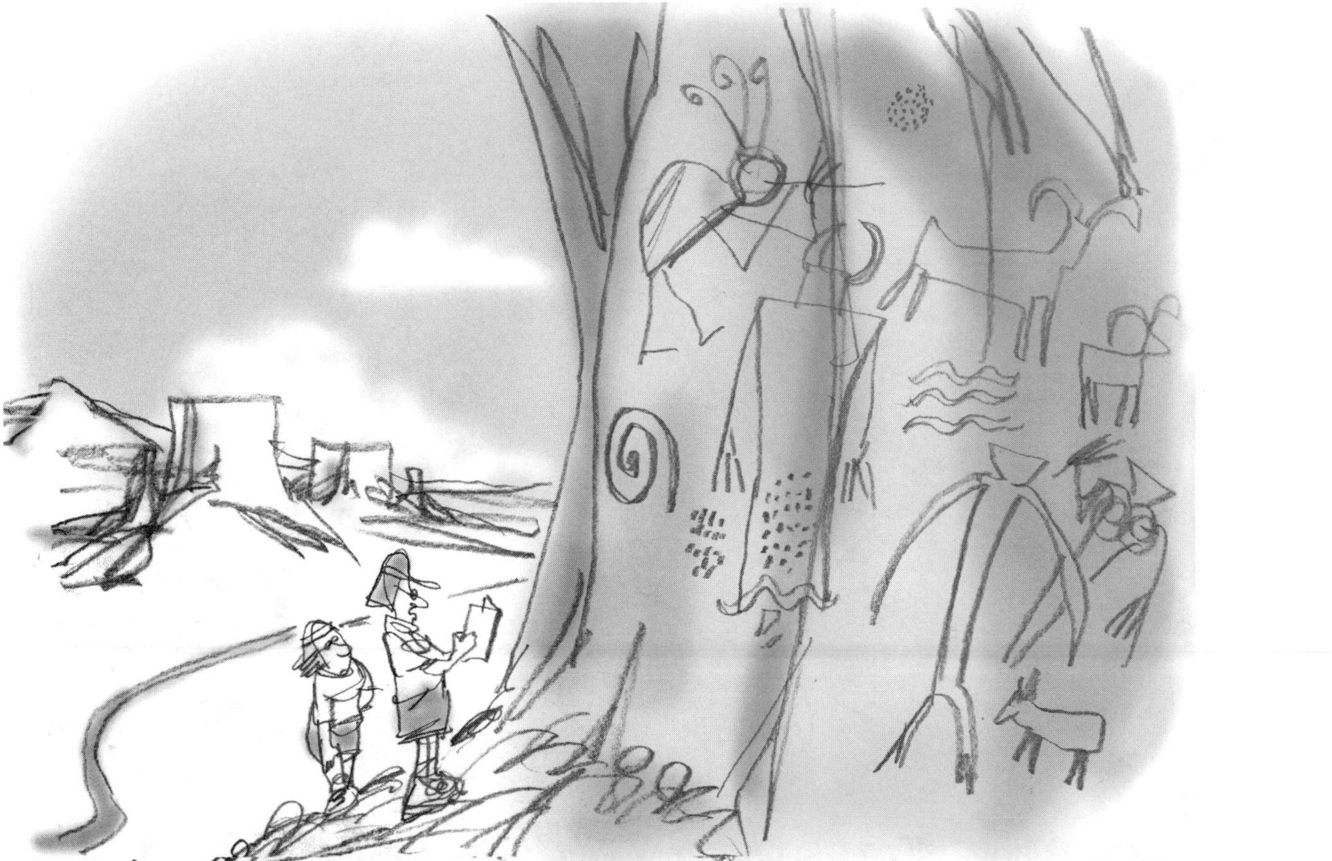

"IT SAYS 'SINGLE, M, ANASAZI, LIKES MUSIC, OUTDOORS, QUIET WALKS IN THE MOONLIGHT, LOOKING TO MYSTERIOUSLY DISAPPEAR WITH THAT SPECIAL SOMEONE.'"

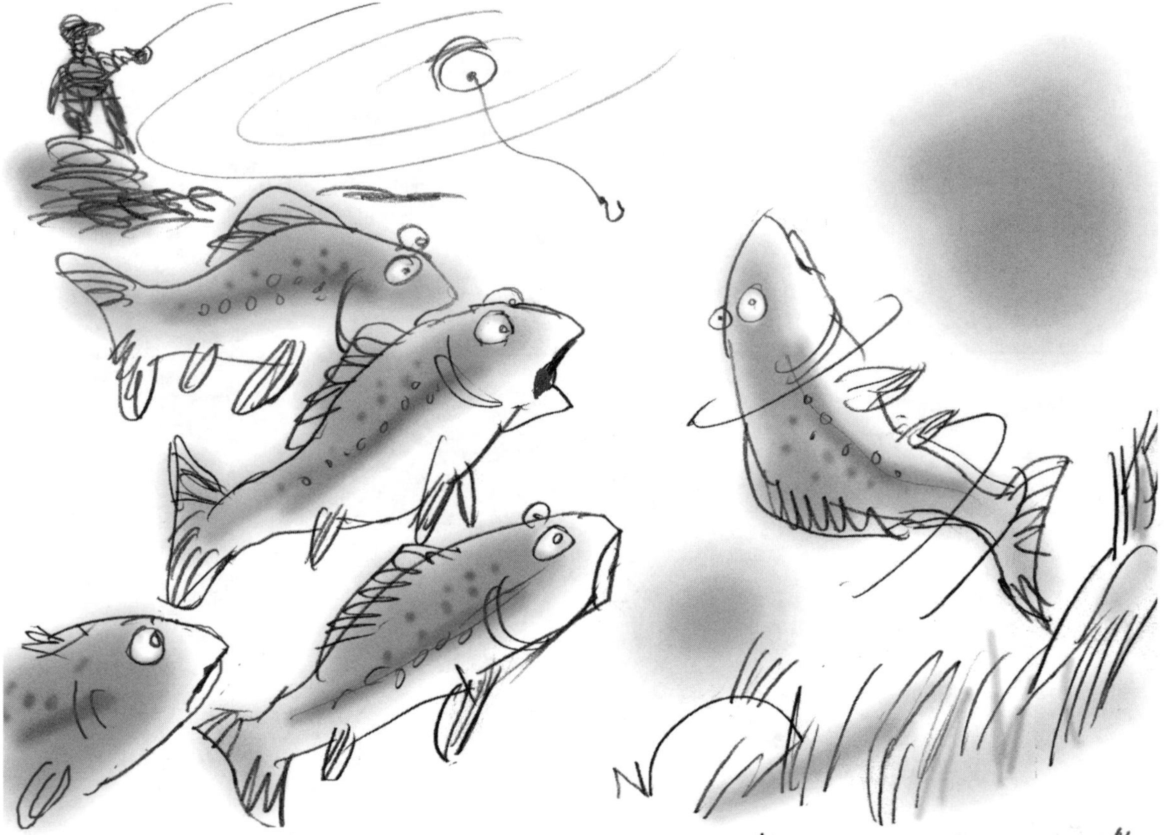

"WE SURE HOPE THAT'S BREAK DANCING YOU'RE DOING THERE, PHIL."

Whirling disease strikes Utah's fisheries.

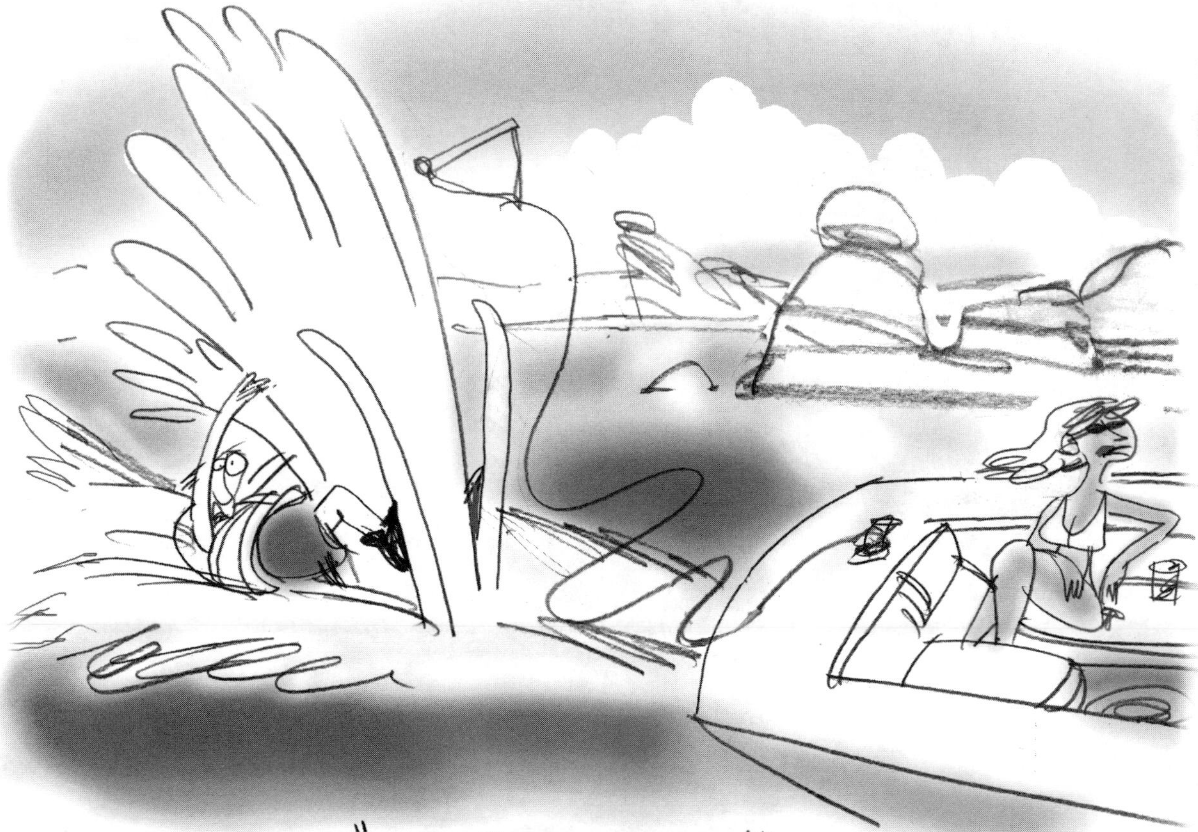

"LAKE POWELL ENEMA!"

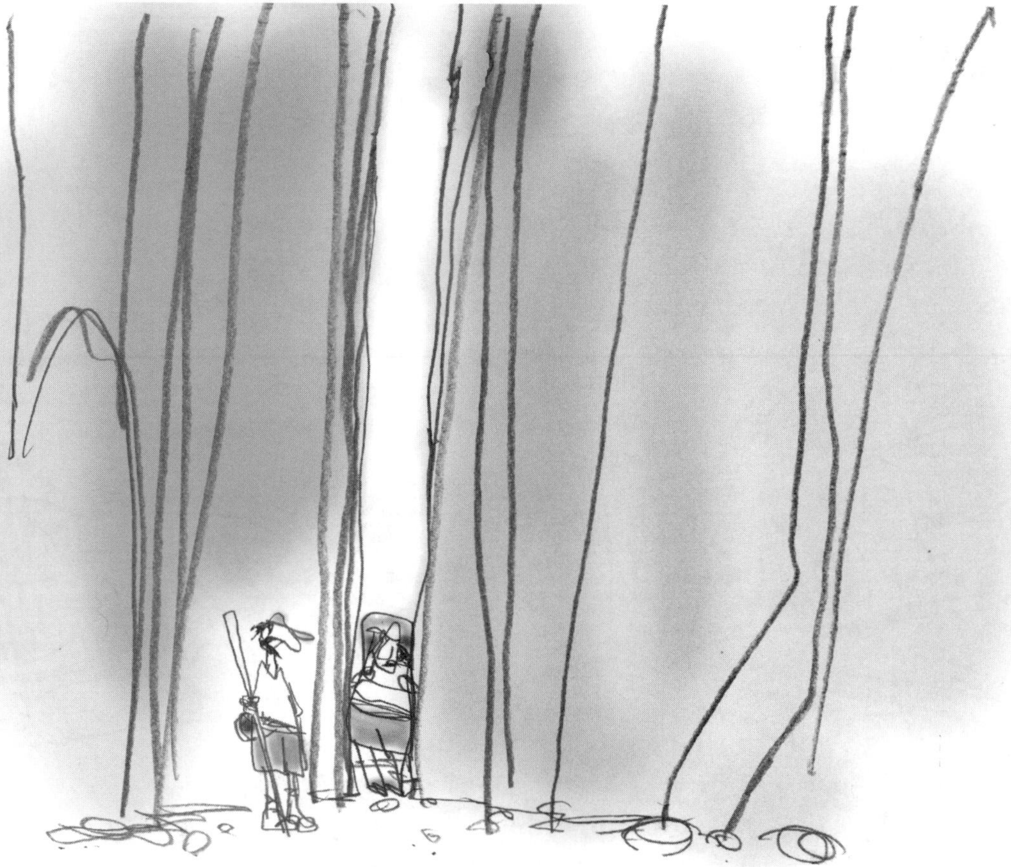

"YOU DIDN'T TELL ME THIS WAS A SIZE 8 SLOT CANYON."

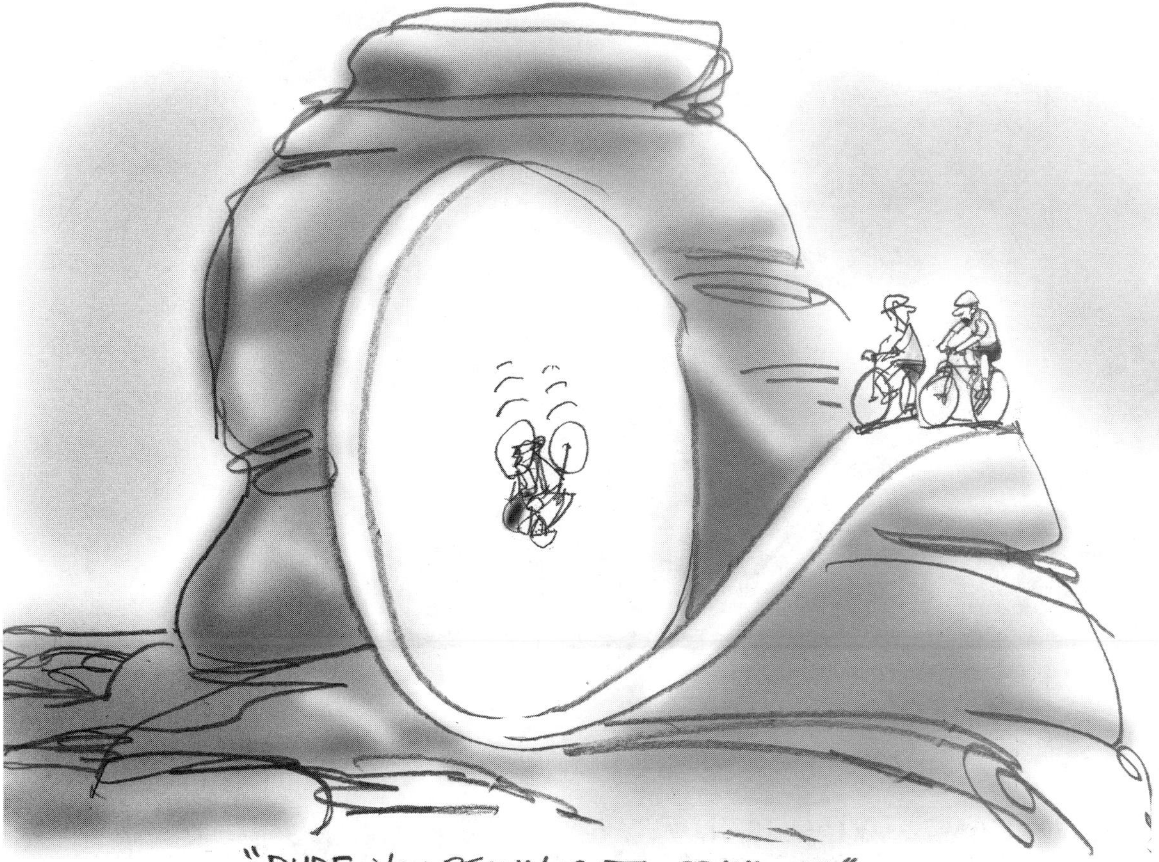

"DUDE, YOU REALLY GOTTA CRANK IT."

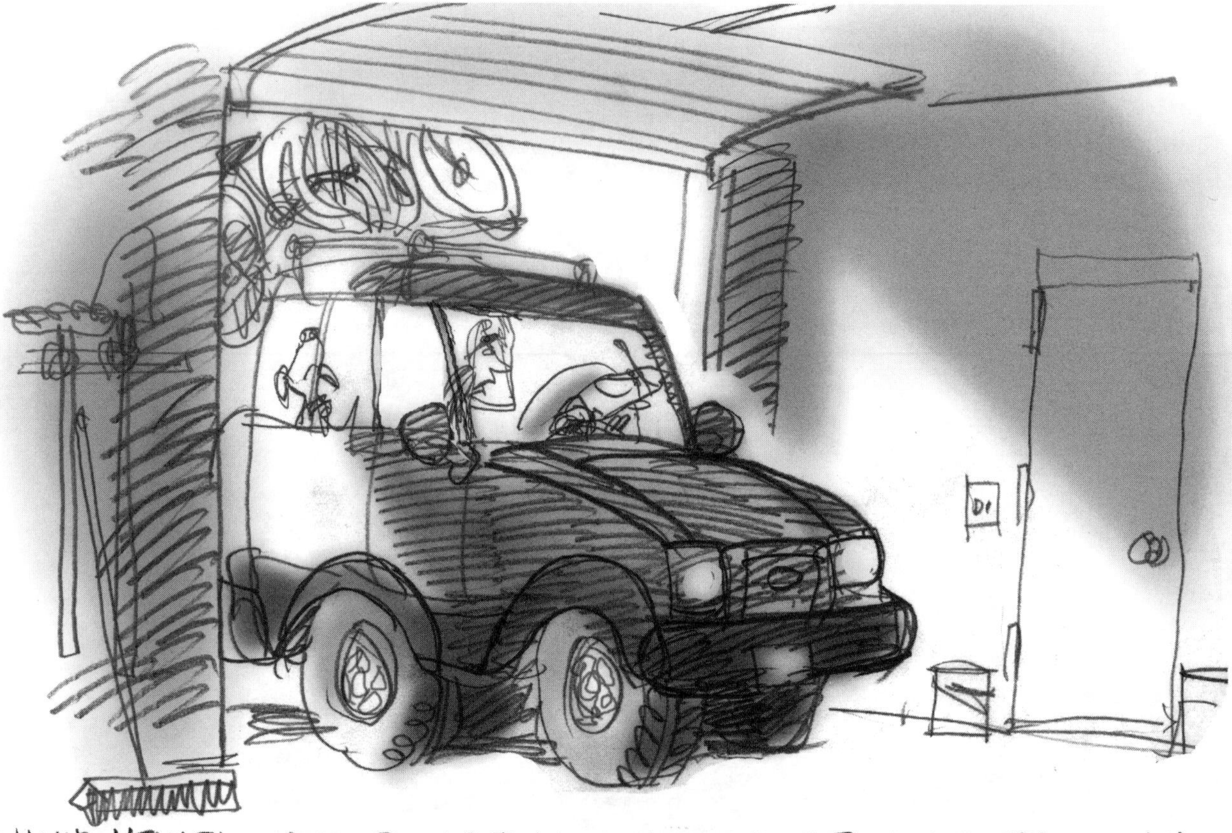

"YOUR NEW THOUSAND-DOLLAR TITANIUM-CARBIDE BIKE FRAME WAS TOUGH ENOUGH TO TAKE WHATEVER MOAB'S RED ROCKS COULD THROW AT IT. BUT MOAB'S RED ROCKS AREN'T AS SMART AS YOU, ARE THEY?"

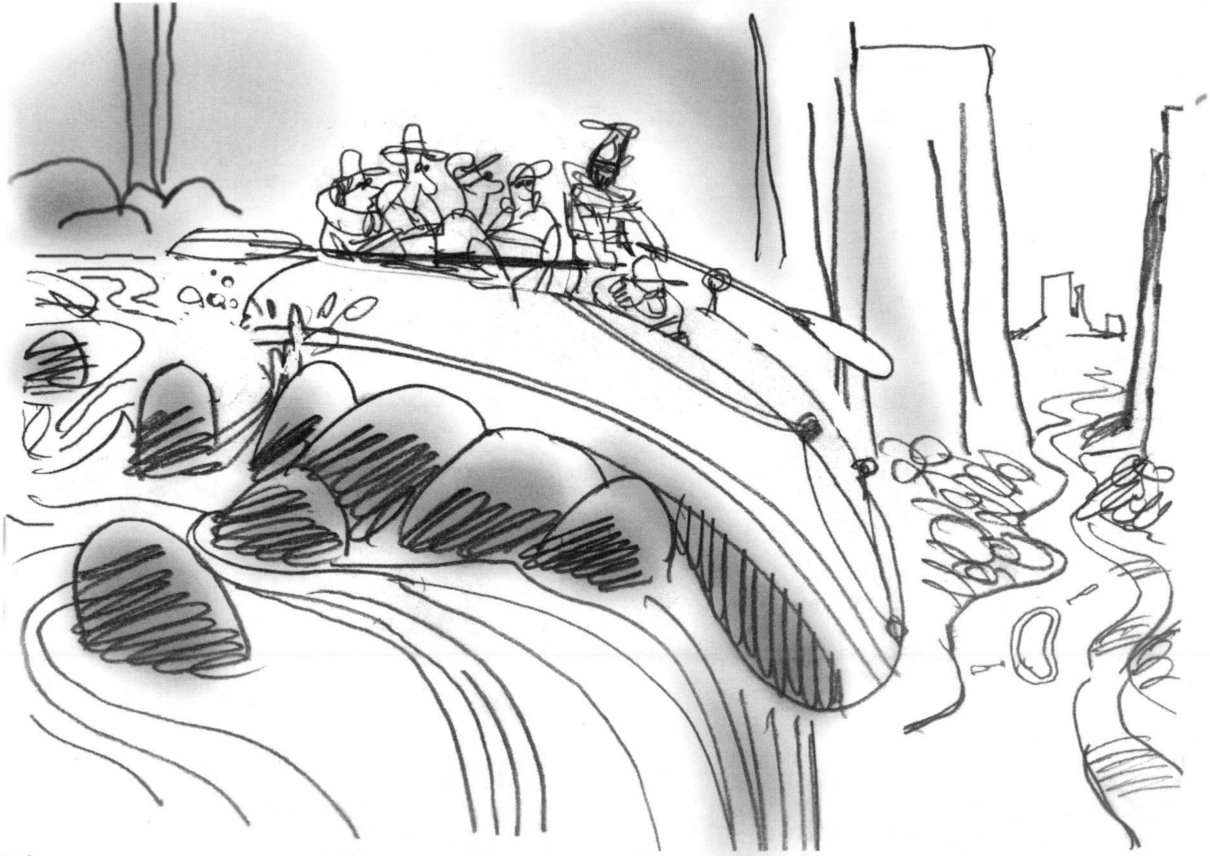

"A ZEN PERSPECTIVE ON THE UNIVERSE COMES IN REAL HANDY RIGHT ABOUT NOW."

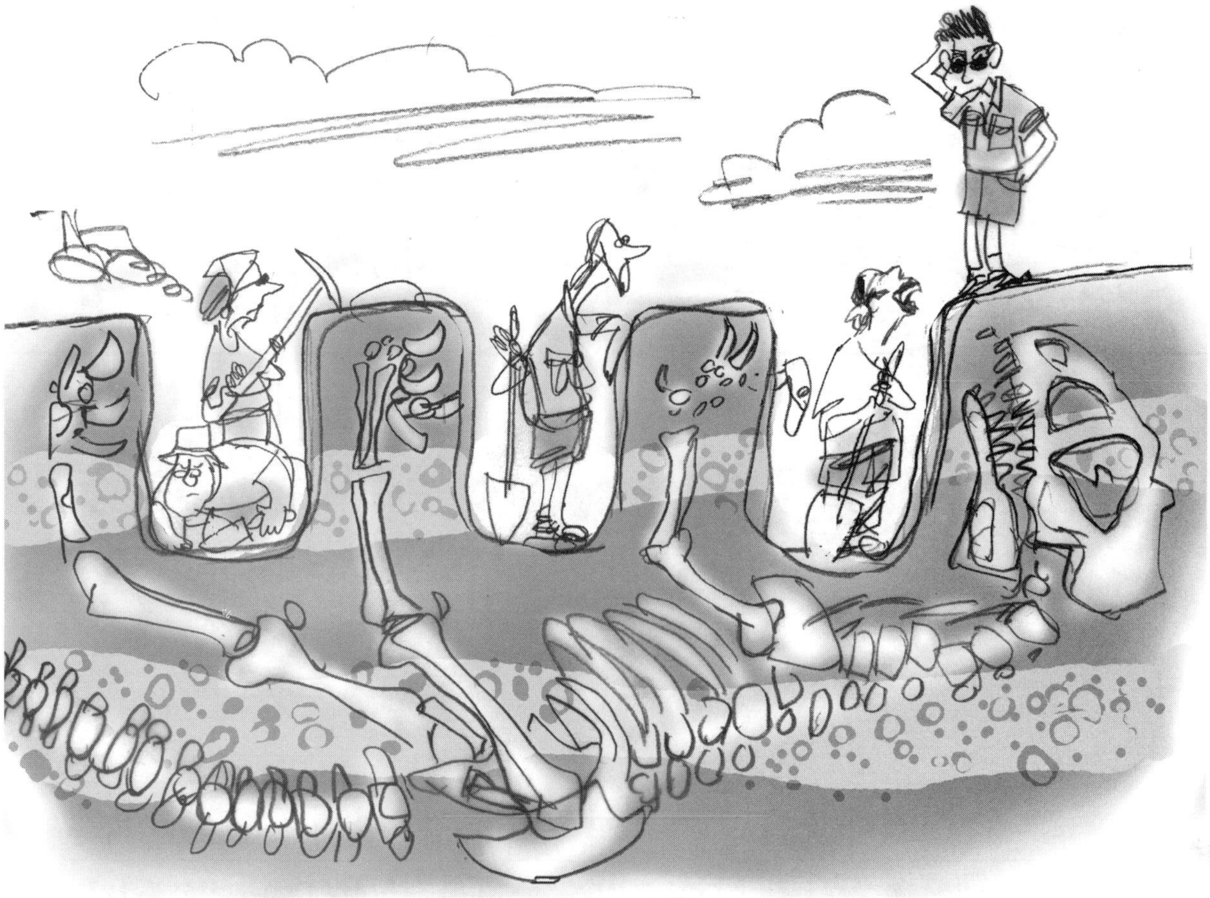

"NOTHING."

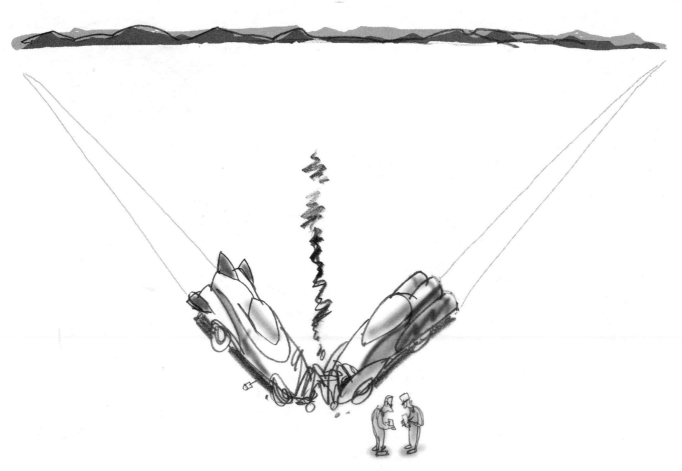

The Salt Flats.

41

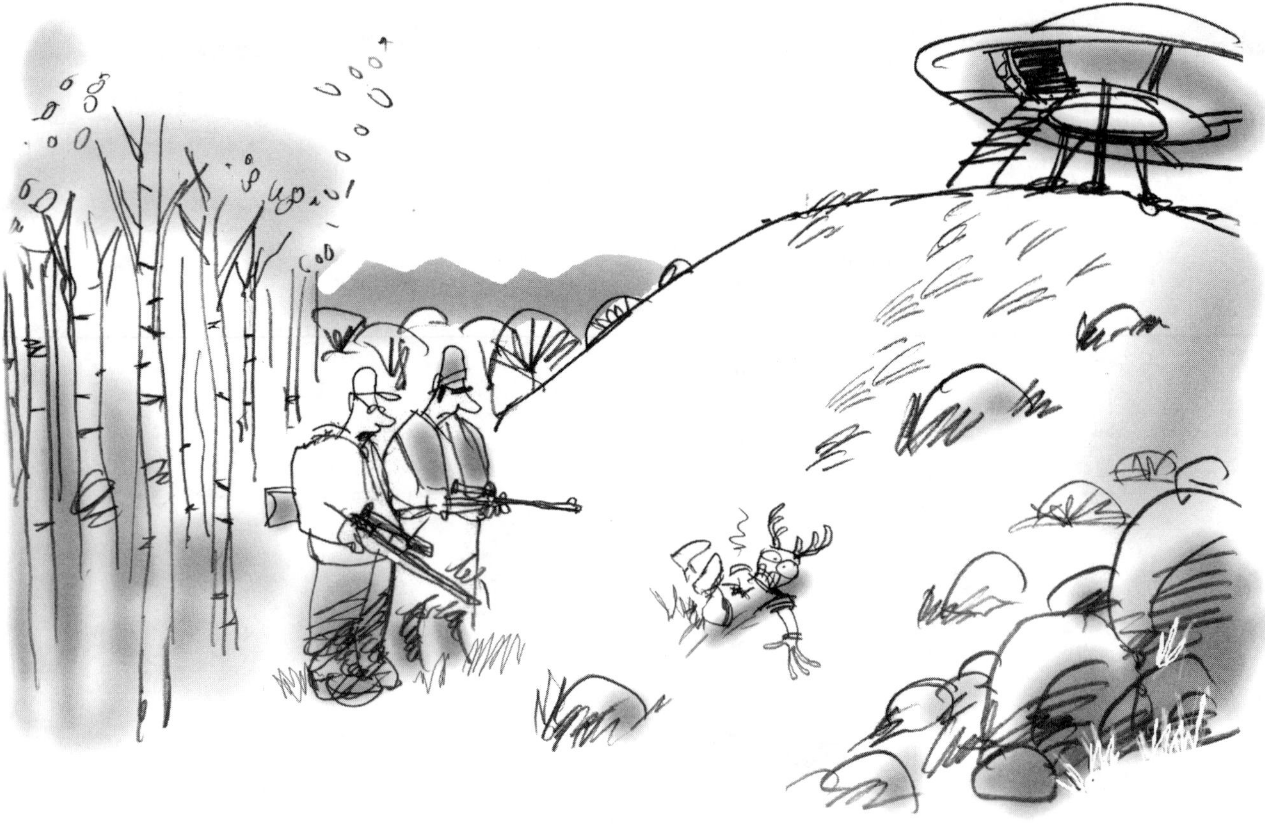

"THAT WAS UNFORTUNATE."

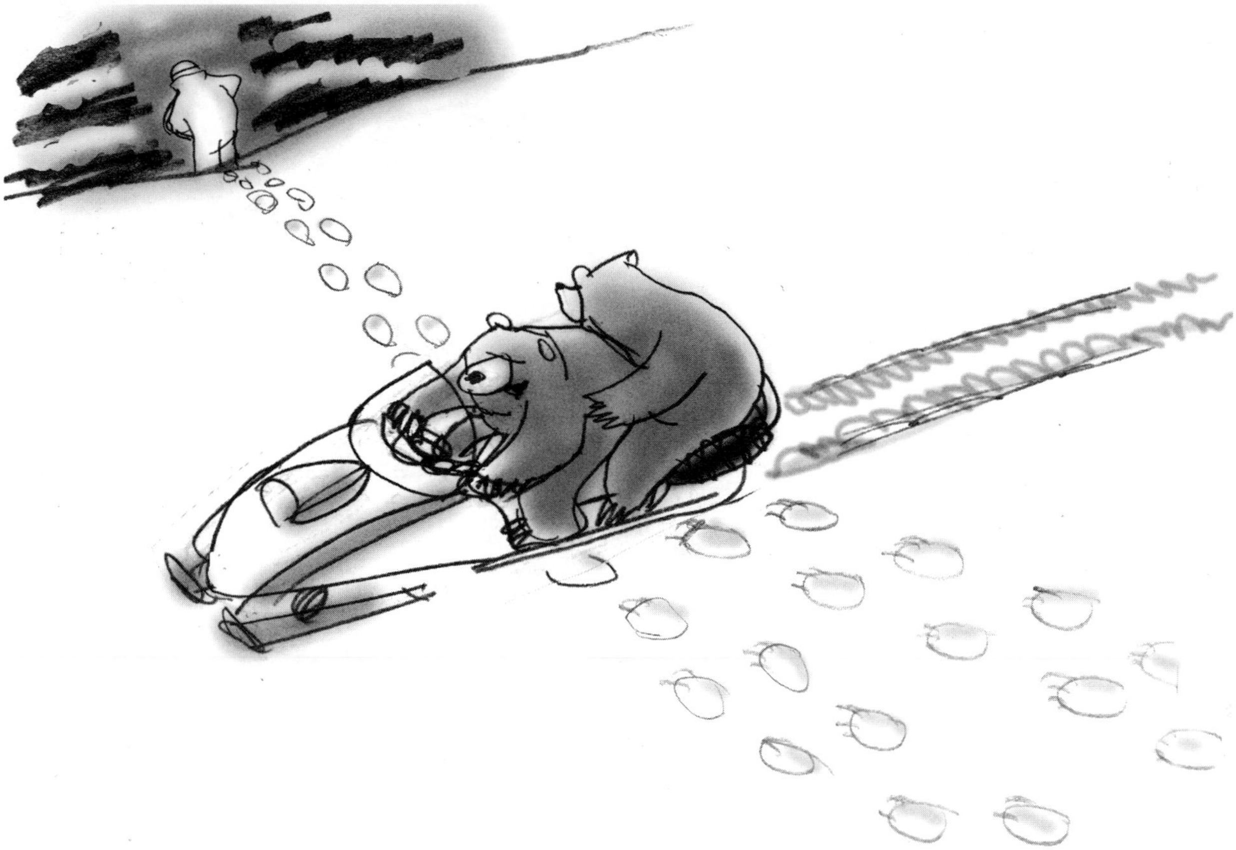

"HANG ON, BABY, PAPA BEAR'S GONNA TAKE YOU FOR THE RIDE OF YOUR LIFE."

I think the Lord himself likes a joke.
If he didn't he wouldn't have made some of you folks.

—J. Golden Kimball

Religious *Utah*

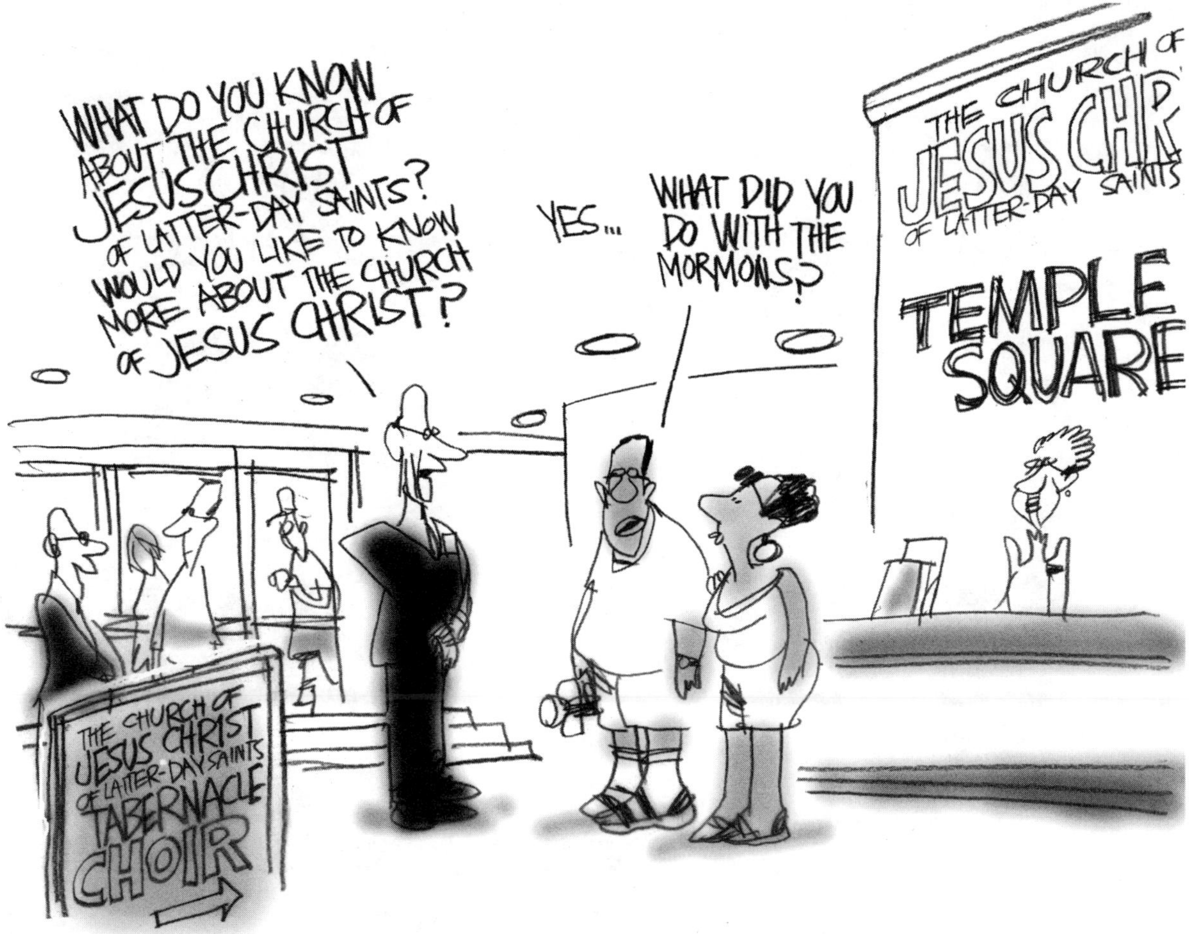
WHAT DO YOU KNOW ABOUT THE CHURCH OF JESUS CHRIST OF LATTER-DAY SAINTS? WOULD YOU LIKE TO KNOW MORE ABOUT THE CHURCH OF JESUS CHRIST?
YES...
WHAT DID YOU DO WITH THE MORMONS?
THE CHURCH OF JESUS CHR OF LATTER-DAY SAINTS
TEMPLE SQUARE
THE CHURCH OF JESUS CHRIST OF LATTER-DAY SAINTS TABERNACLE CHOIR

The Church wants to be identified by its Christian name.

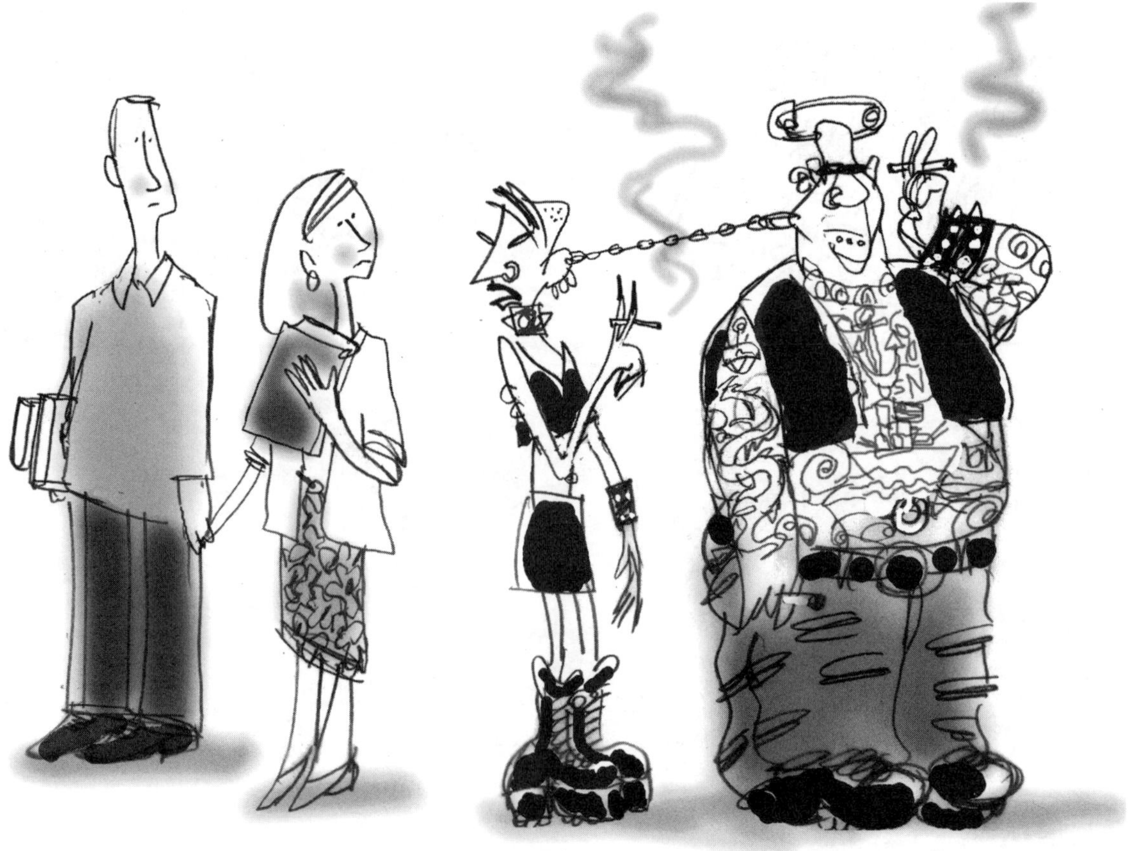

"YOU MORMONS ARE SO BIZARRE!"

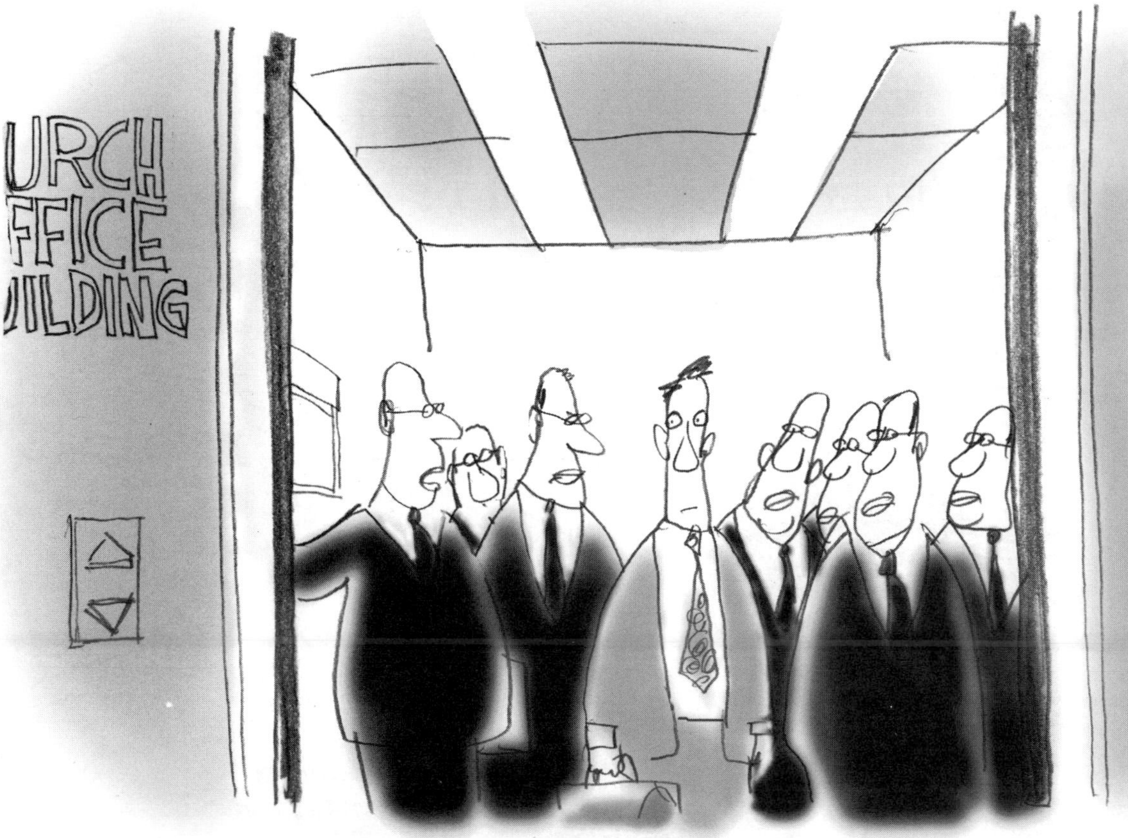
URCH
FFICE
UILDING

"BROTHER HENDERSON–THINKING OUTSIDE THE BOX AGAIN, ARE WE?"

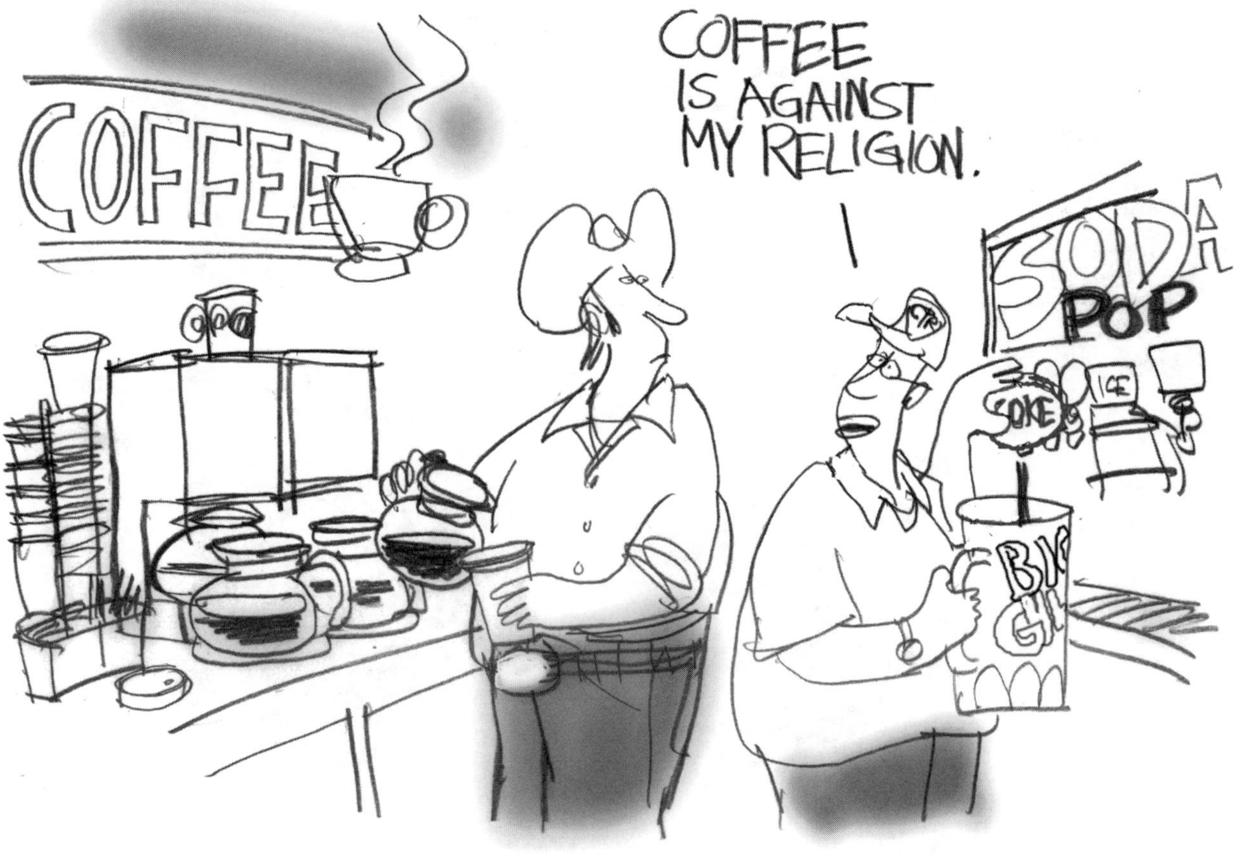
COFFEE
COFFEE IS AGAINST MY RELIGION.
SODA
POP
ICE
COKE

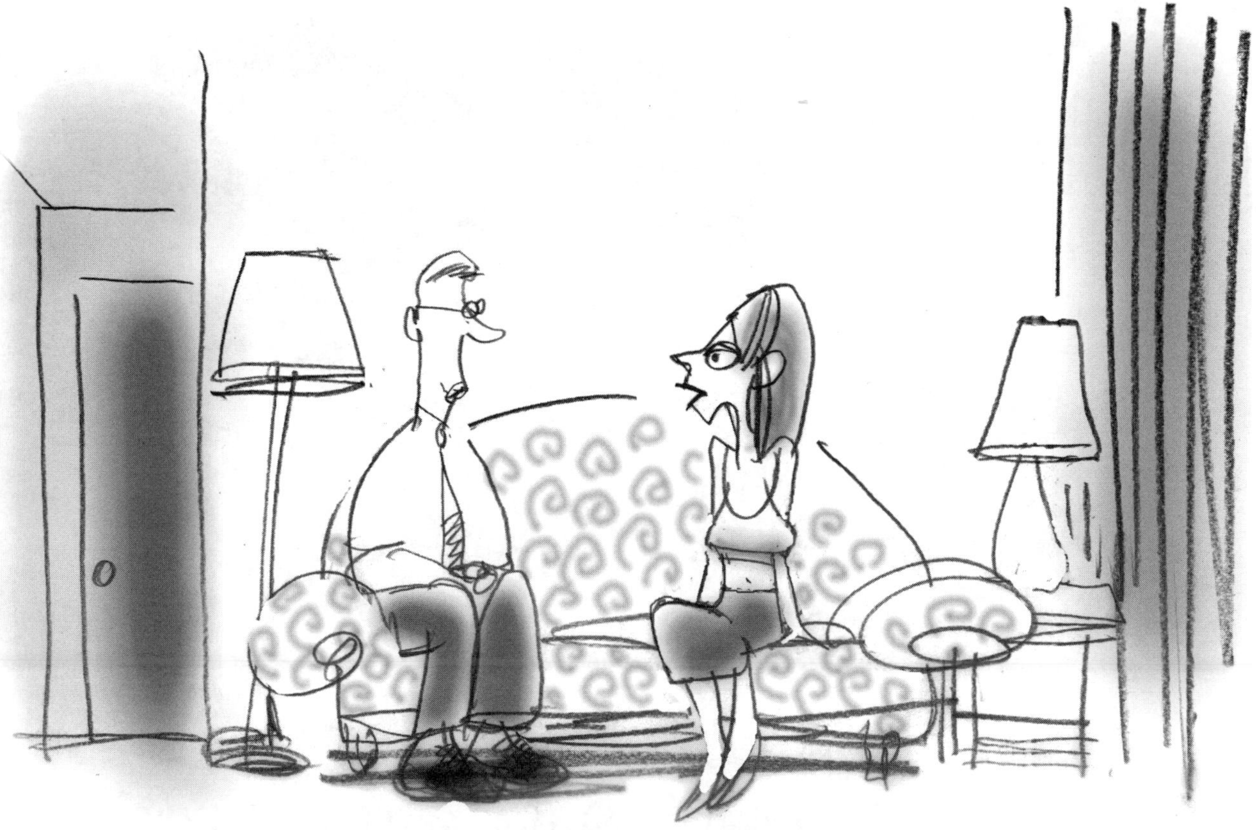

"SURE I WANT SOMEONE WHO CAN TAKE ME TO THE CELESTIAL KINGDOM—PREFERABLY BY WAY OF FEDERAL HEIGHTS."

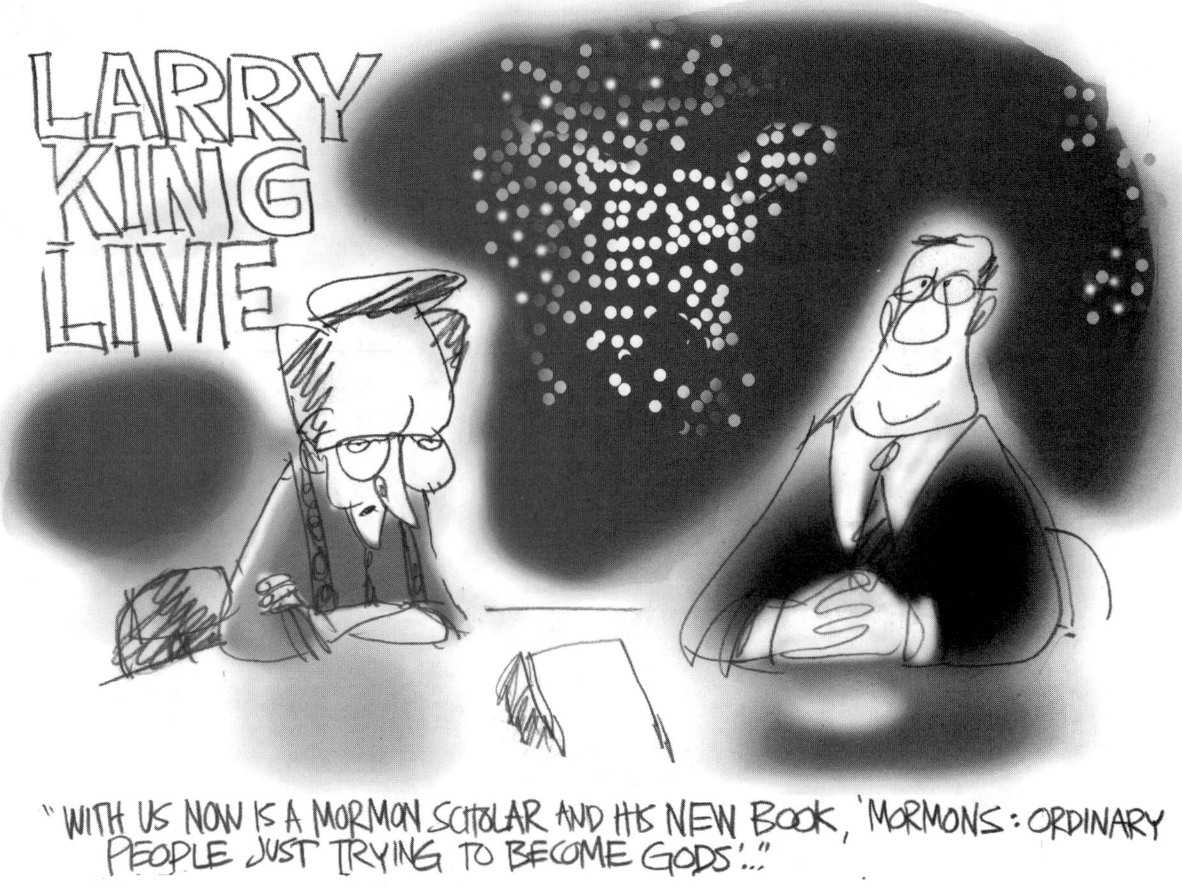
LARRY KING LIVE
"WITH US NOW IS A MORMON SCHOLAR AND HIS NEW BOOK, 'MORMONS: ORDINARY PEOPLE JUST TRYING TO BECOME GODS'..."

On national TV, Larry King grilled LDS President Gordon B. Hinkley on early Mormon polygamy. This from a man who has been married seven times.

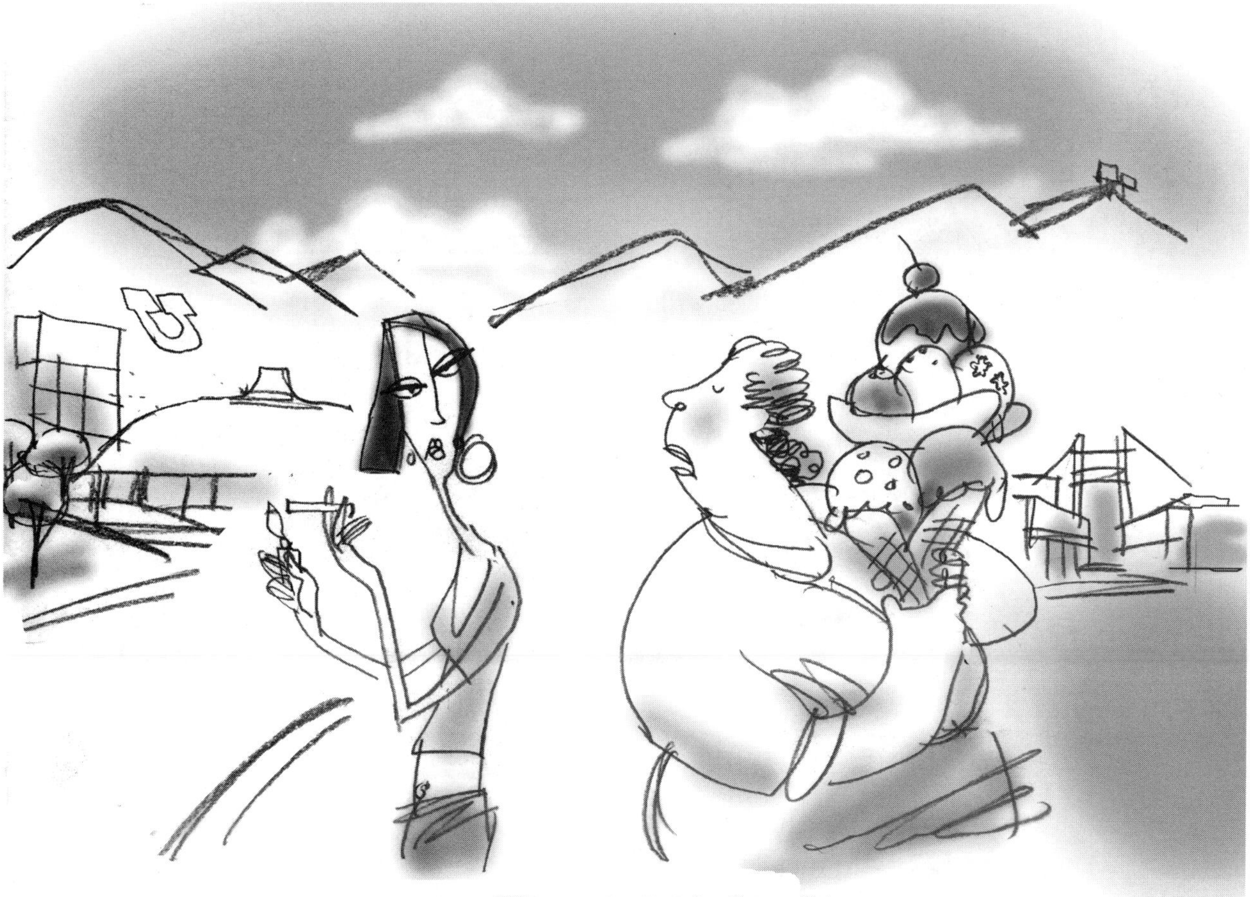

"IT'S YOUR FUNERAL."

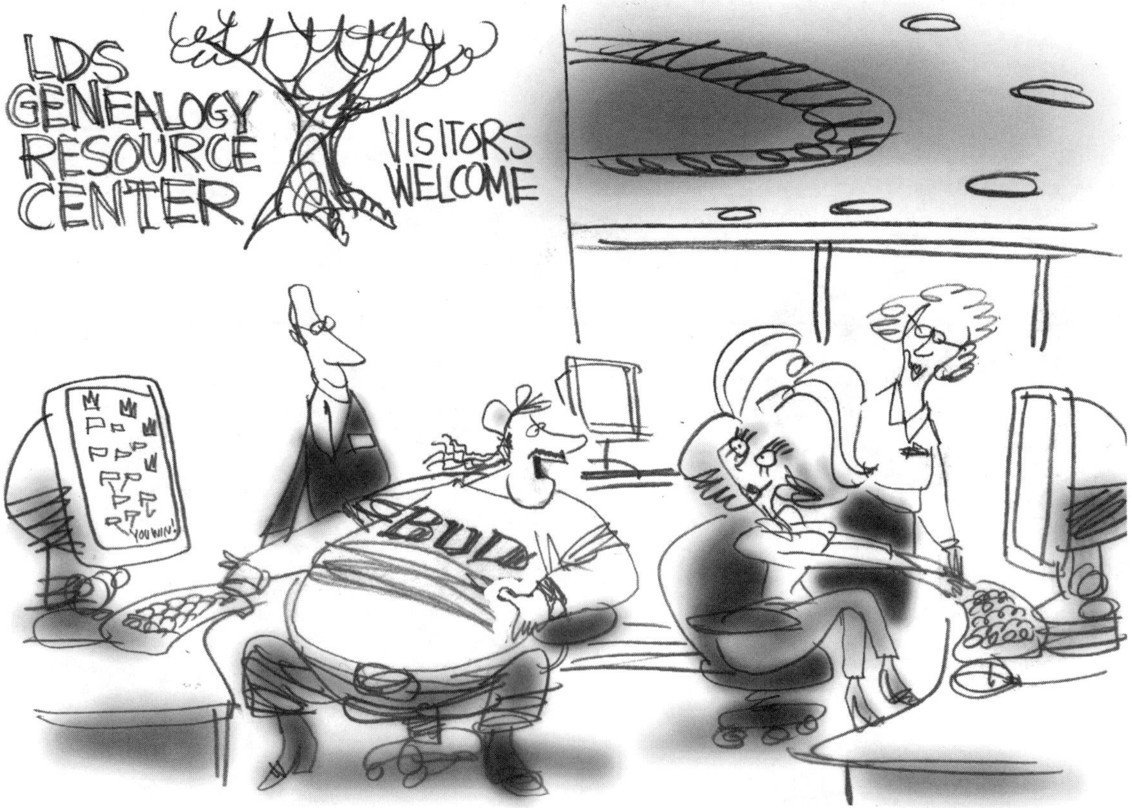
LDS GENEALOGY RESOURCE CENTER
VISITORS WELCOME
BUD
YOU WIN!

"LOOKY HERE, BABY-DOLL—I'M RELATED TO ROYALTY."

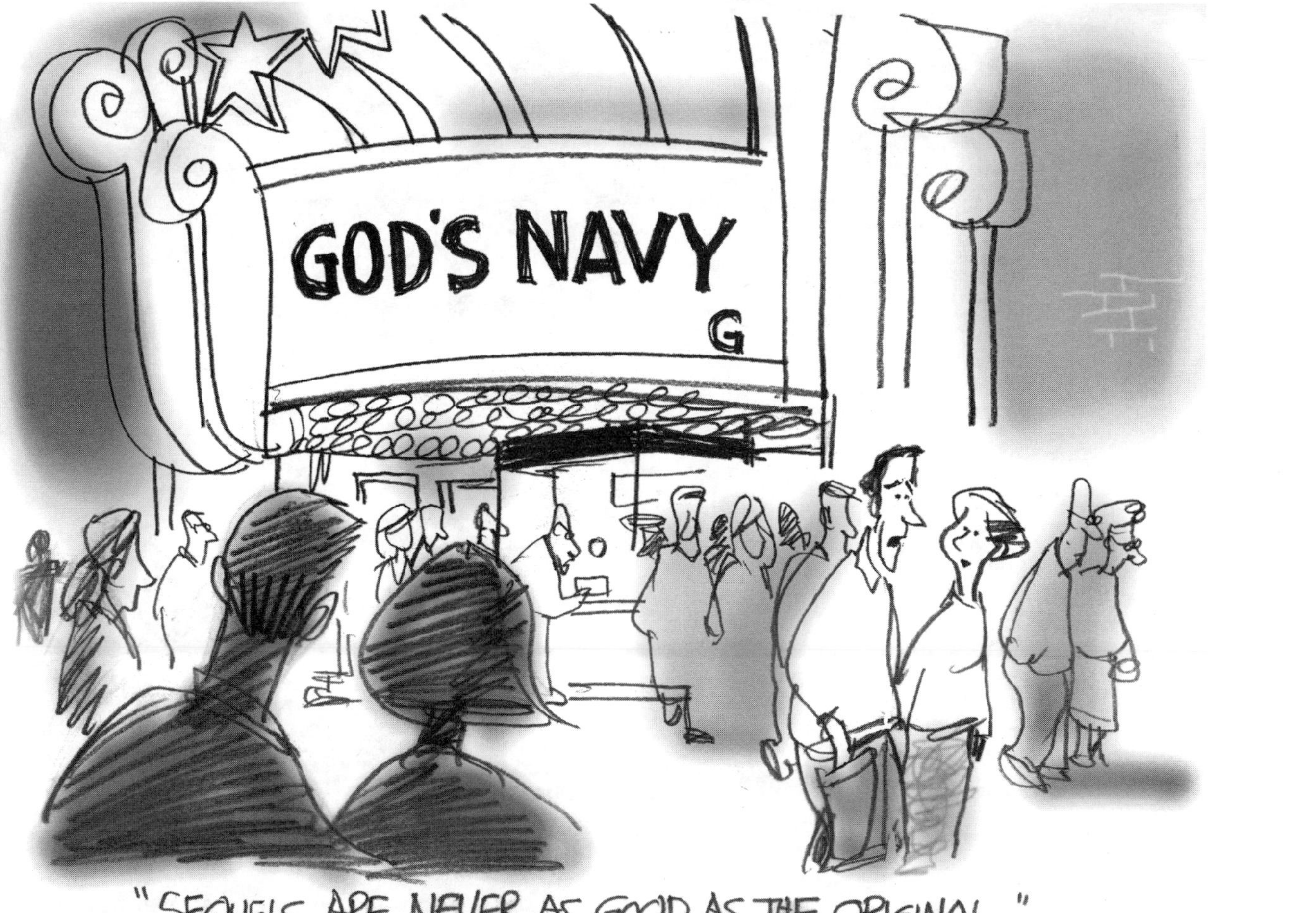
GOD'S NAVY
G

"SEQUELS ARE NEVER AS GOOD AS THE ORIGINAL."

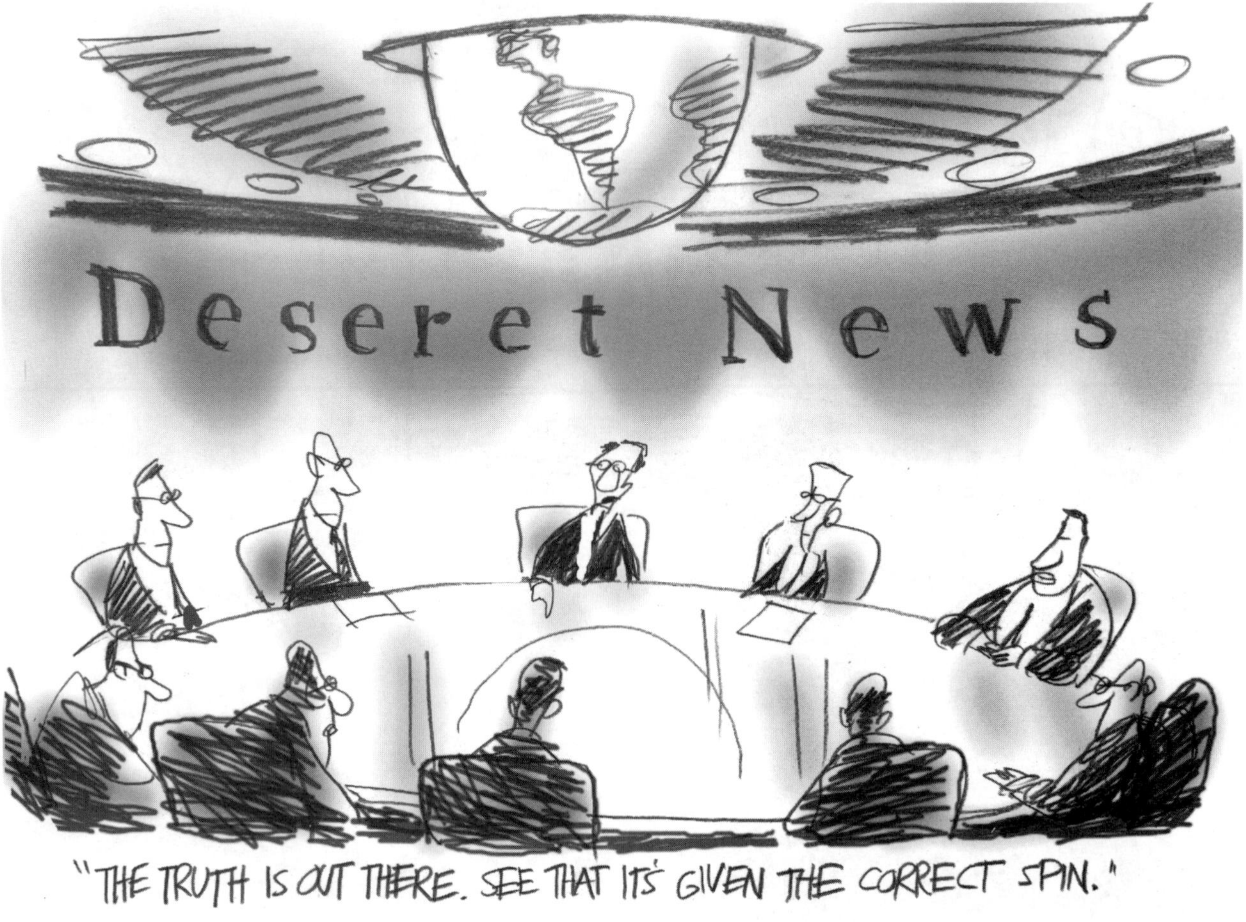
Deseret News
"THE TRUTH IS OUT THERE. SEE THAT IT'S GIVEN THE CORRECT SPIN."

I should disclose to the reader that I may be unfairly biased as I work for the Deseret News' *competitor. Thank God.*

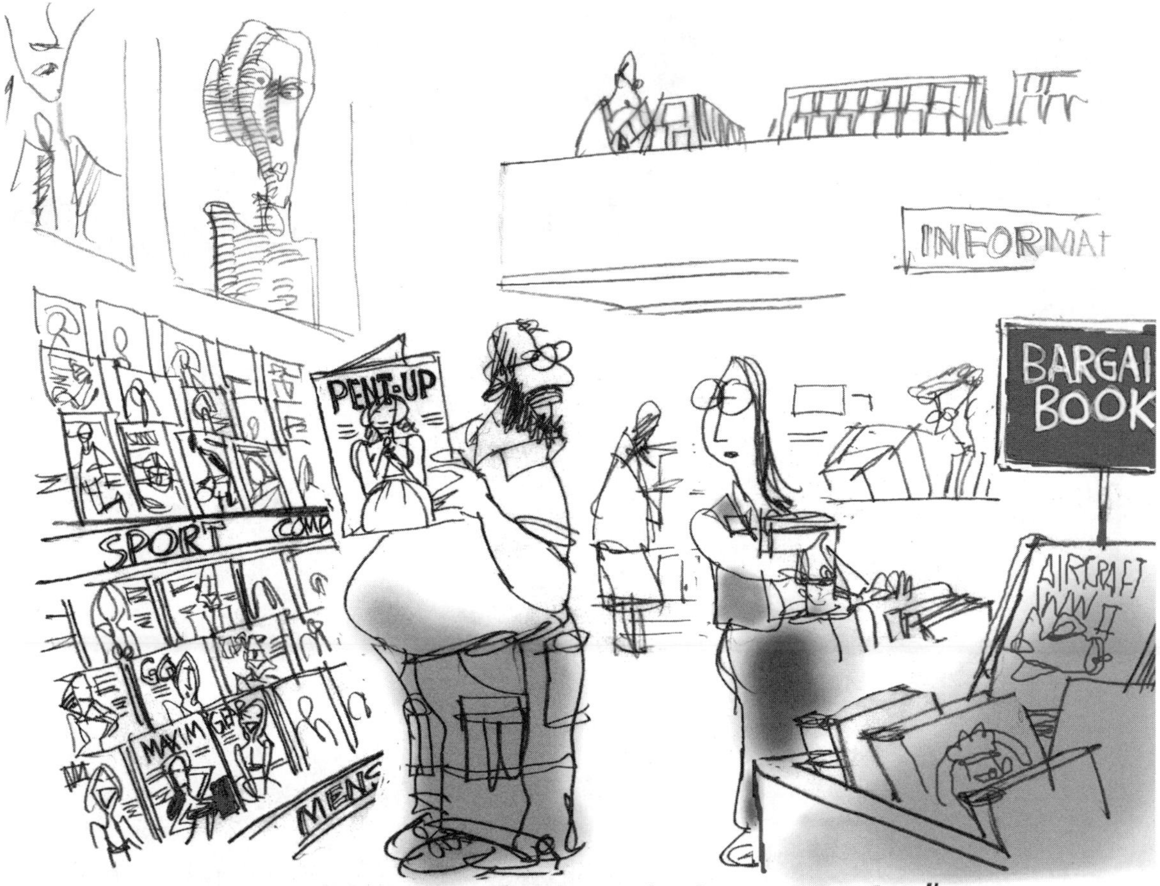
PENT-UP
SPORT
COMP
MAXIM
GQ
MENS
INFORMA
BARGAI
BOOK
AIRCRAFT
WW II

" IT'S A NEW MAGAZINE FOR MORMON SINGLES."

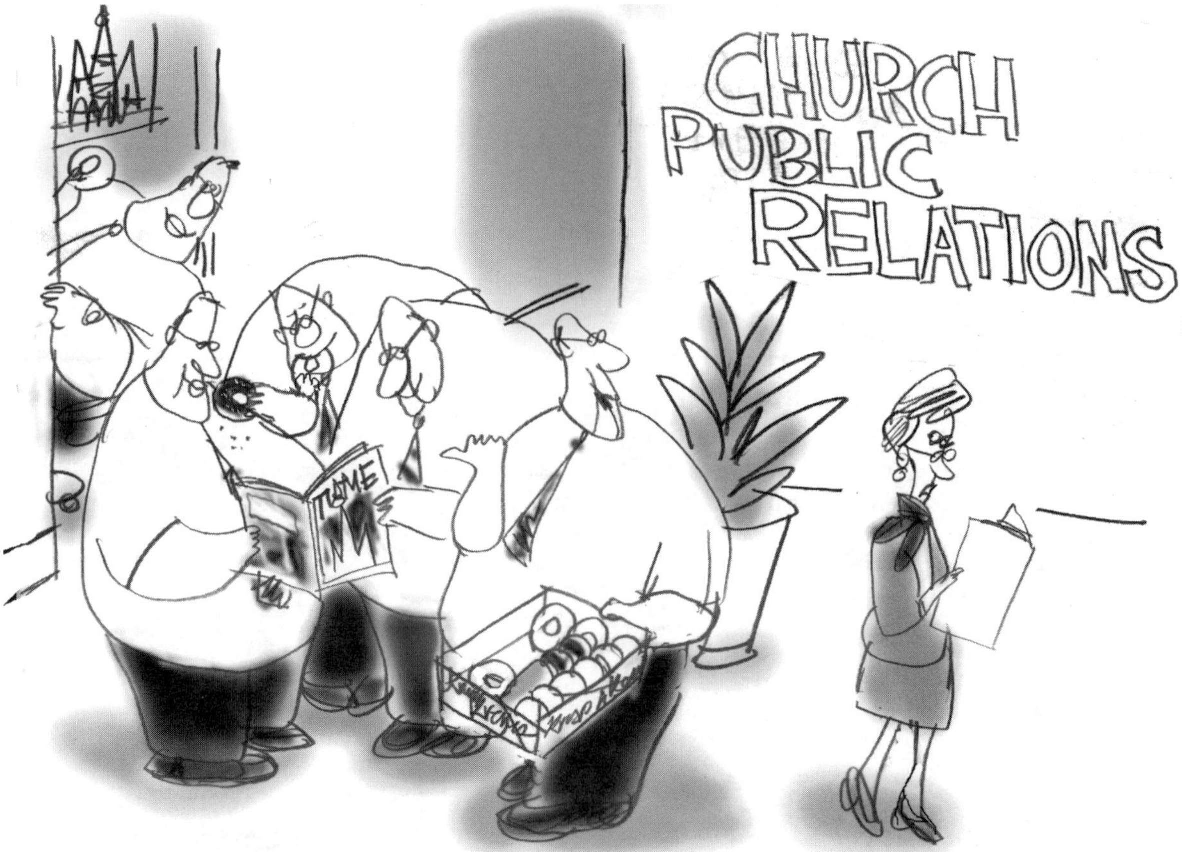
CHURCH
PUBLIC
RELATIONS
TIME

"IT SAYS WE'RE THE MOST RAPIDLY EXPANDING RELIGIOUS ORGANIZATION IN THE WORLD!"

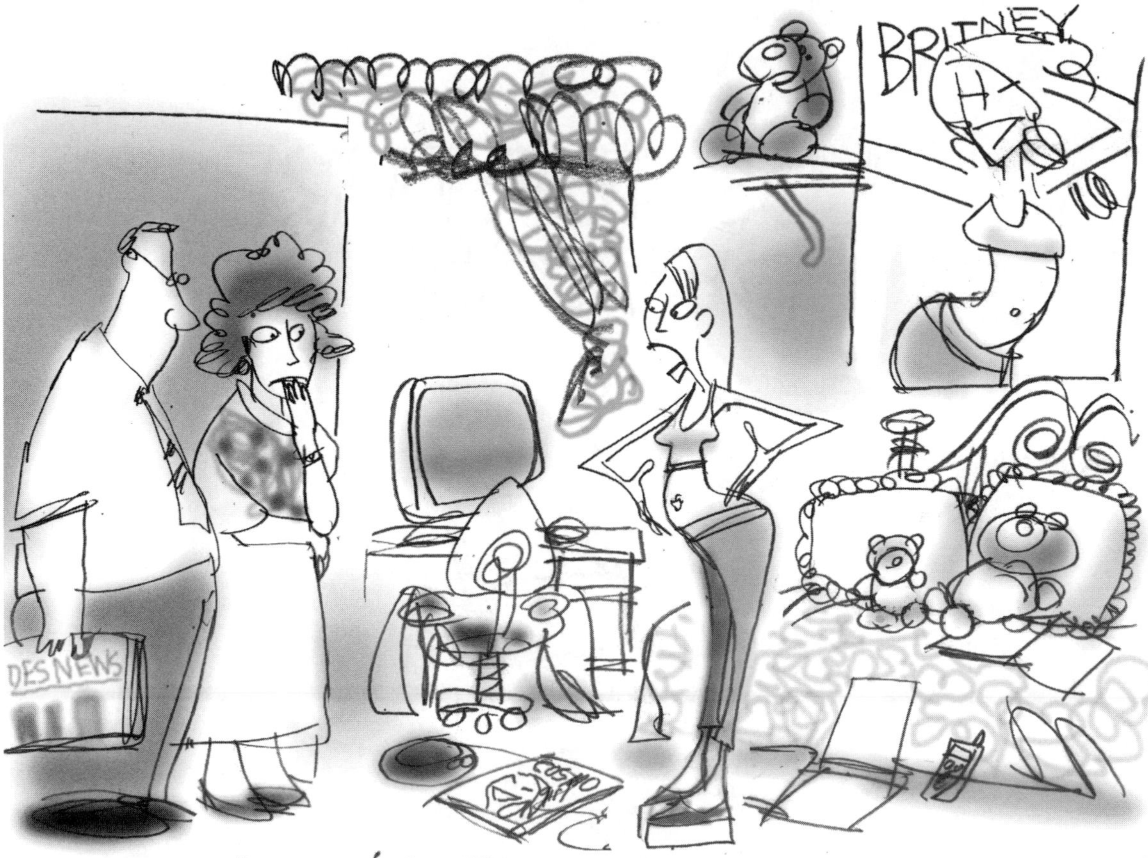
BRITNEY
DES NEWS
COSMO
"BUT IT'S A CTR BELLYBUTTON RING!"

CTR stands for Choose the Right. The stylized initials are popular in LDS jewelry.

LDS TORTURE DEVICE

Also popular with other long-winded Faiths.

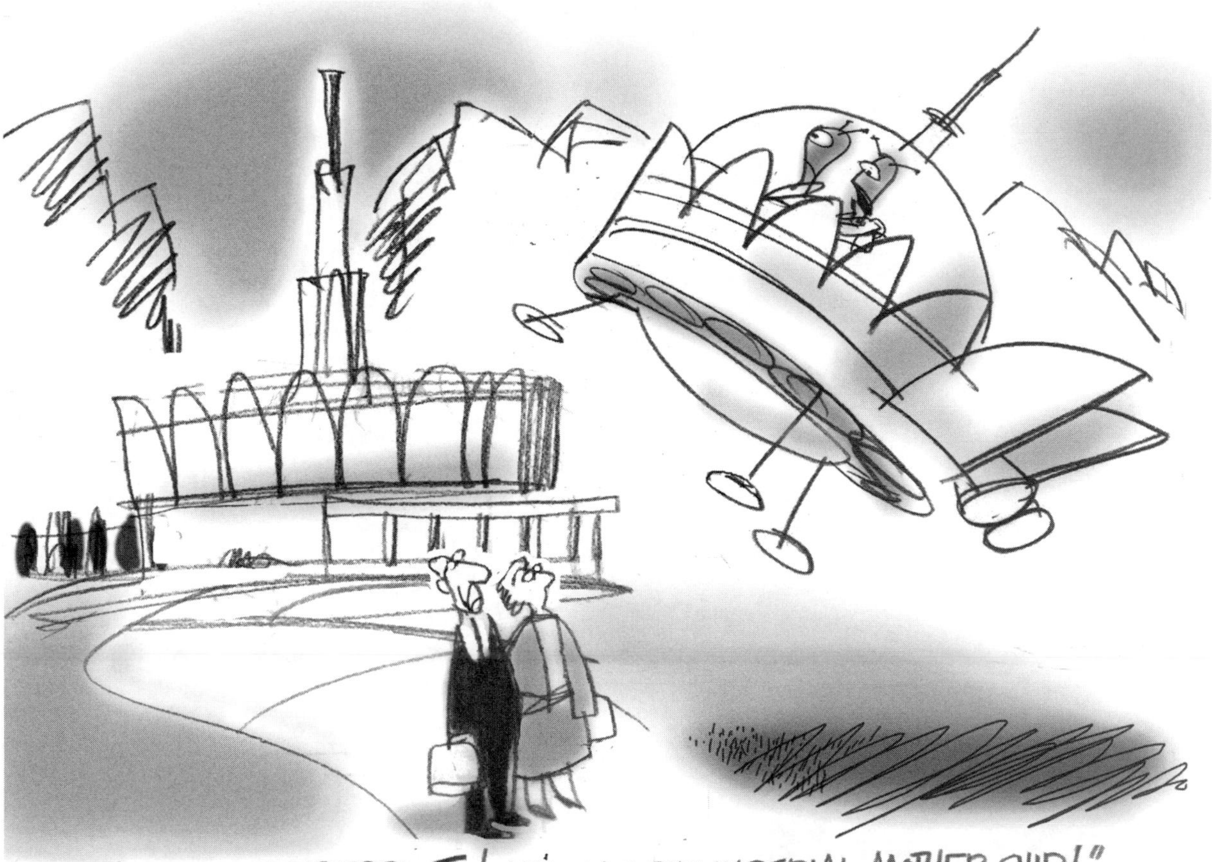

"PULL UP, ZERBLOT! IT'S NOT THE IMPERIAL MOTHER SHIP!"

Let's call it a benevolent despotism.

—Wallace Stegner

Political *Utah*

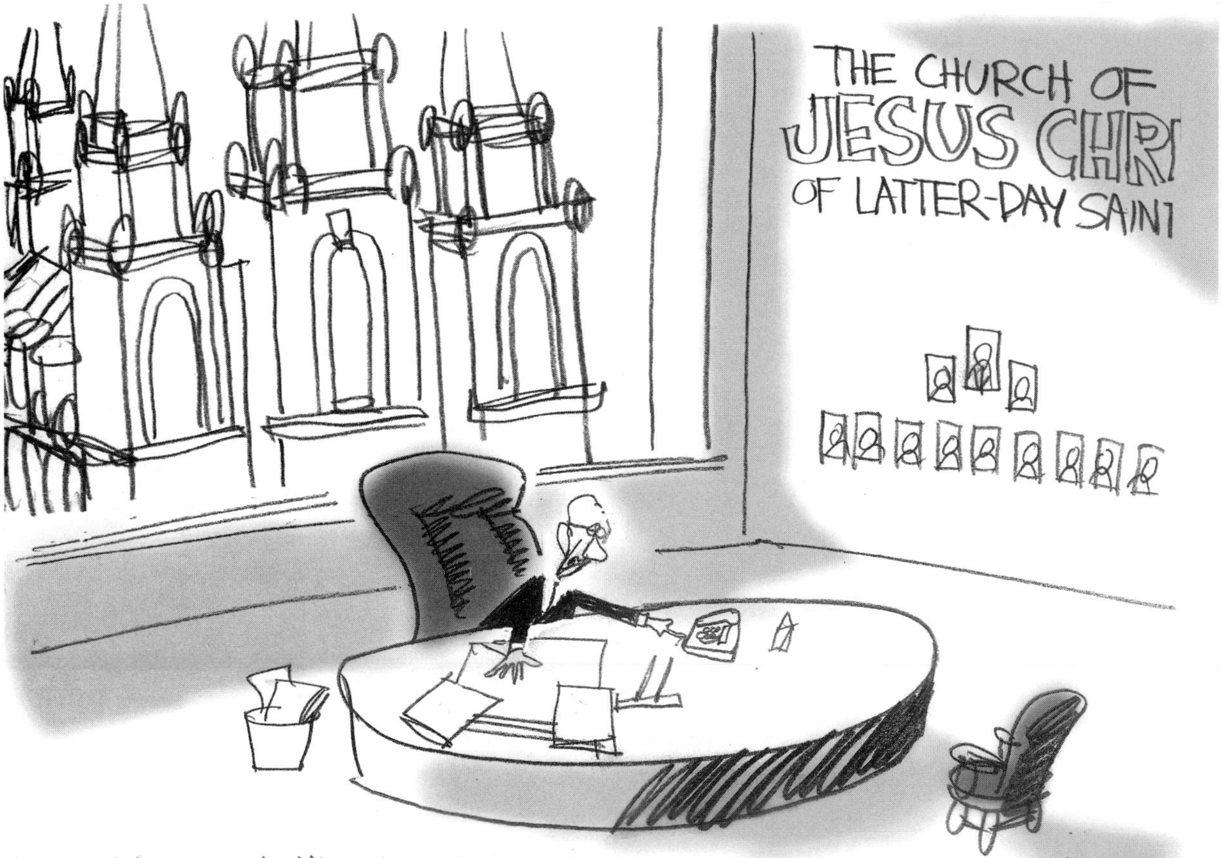
THE CHURCH OF
JESUS CHRI
OF LATTER-DAY SAINT

"SISTER FINCHLEY – I'M TIRED OF THESE STORIES IN THE MEDIA THAT SAY THE CHURCH CALLS ALL THE SHOTS IN UTAH..., HAVE THE LEGISLATURE PASS A RESOLUTION DENYING IT."

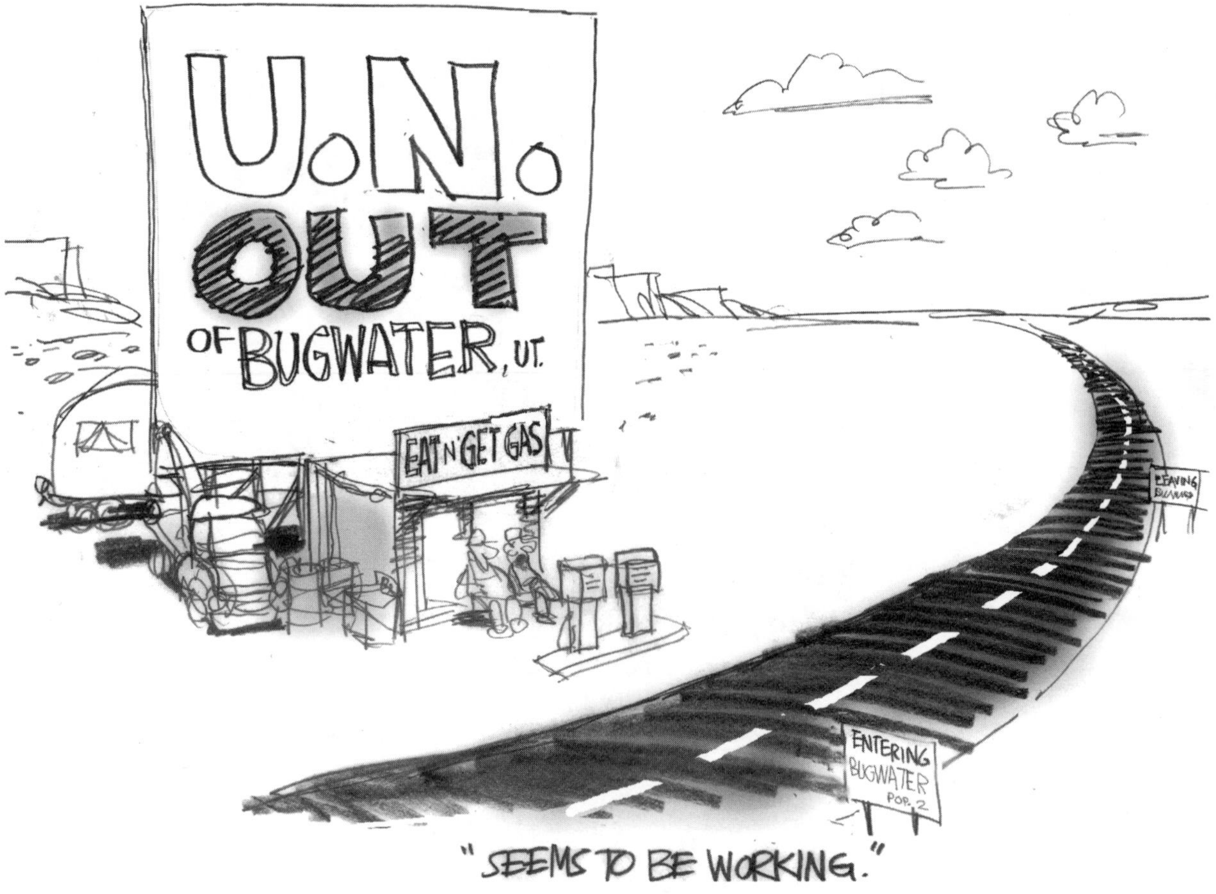

U.N. OUT OF BUGWATER, UT.
EAT N' GET GAS
ENTERING BUGWATER POP. 2
"SEEMS TO BE WORKING."

The city council of the southern Utah community of La Verkin passes a resolution banning the United Nations within city limits.

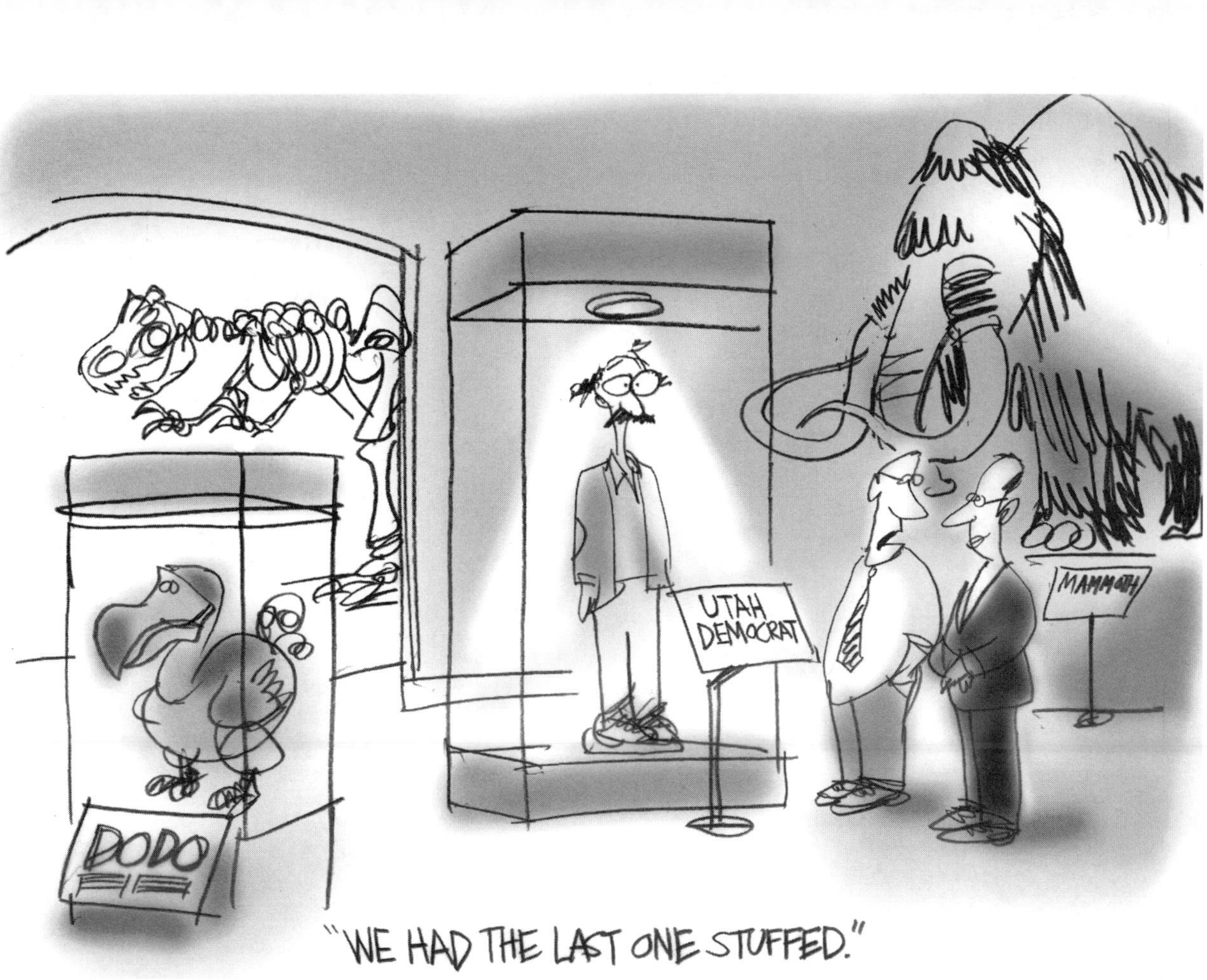
UTAH DEMOCRAT
MAMMOTH
DODO

"WE HAD THE LAST ONE STUFFED."

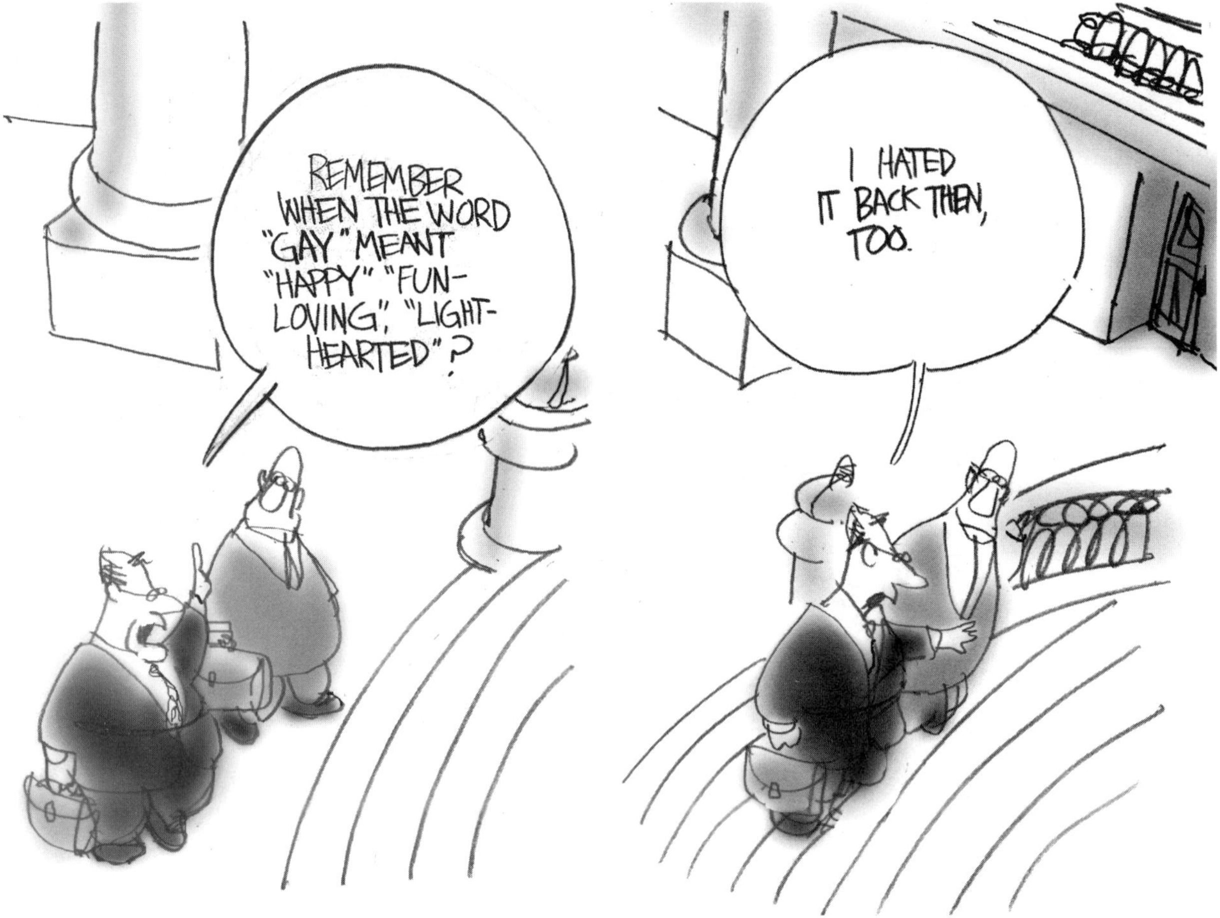
REMEMBER WHEN THE WORD "GAY" MEANT "HAPPY" "FUN-LOVING", "LIGHT-HEARTED"?
I HATED IT BACK THEN, TOO.

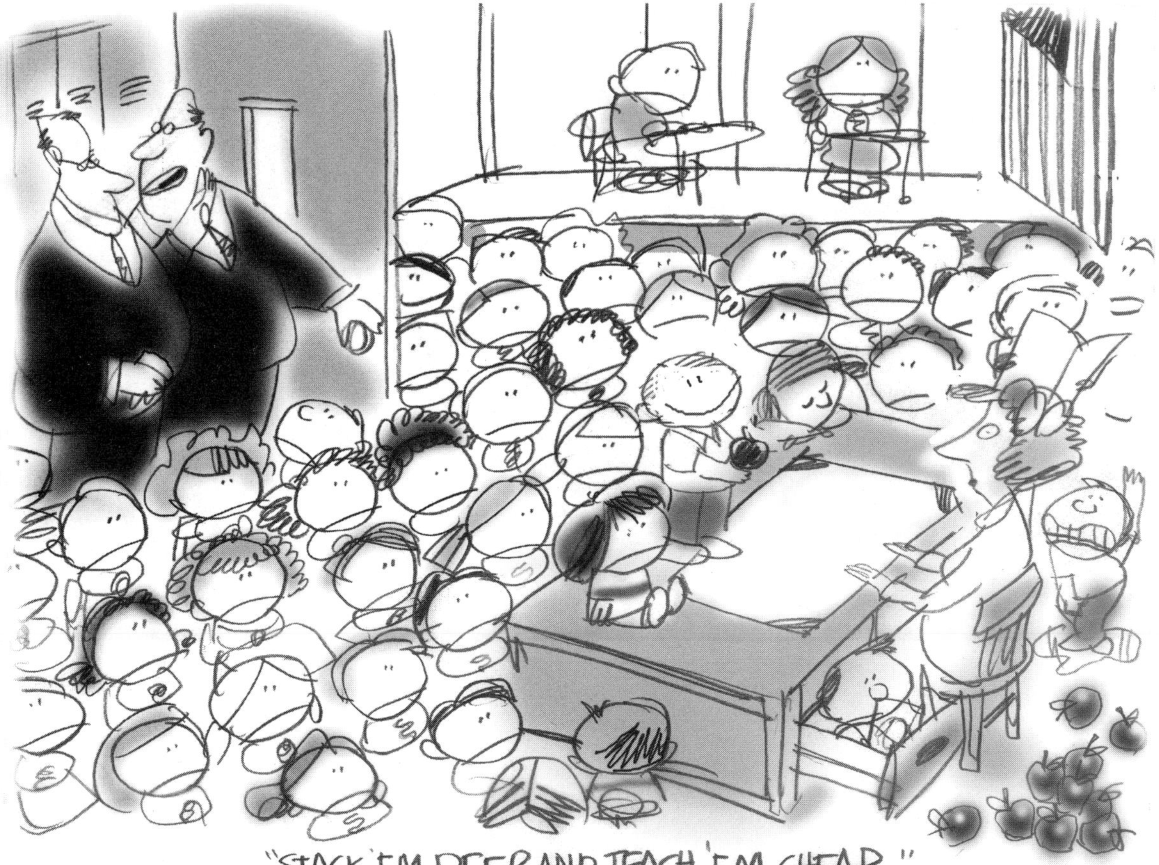

"STACK 'EM DEEP AND TEACH 'EM CHEAP."

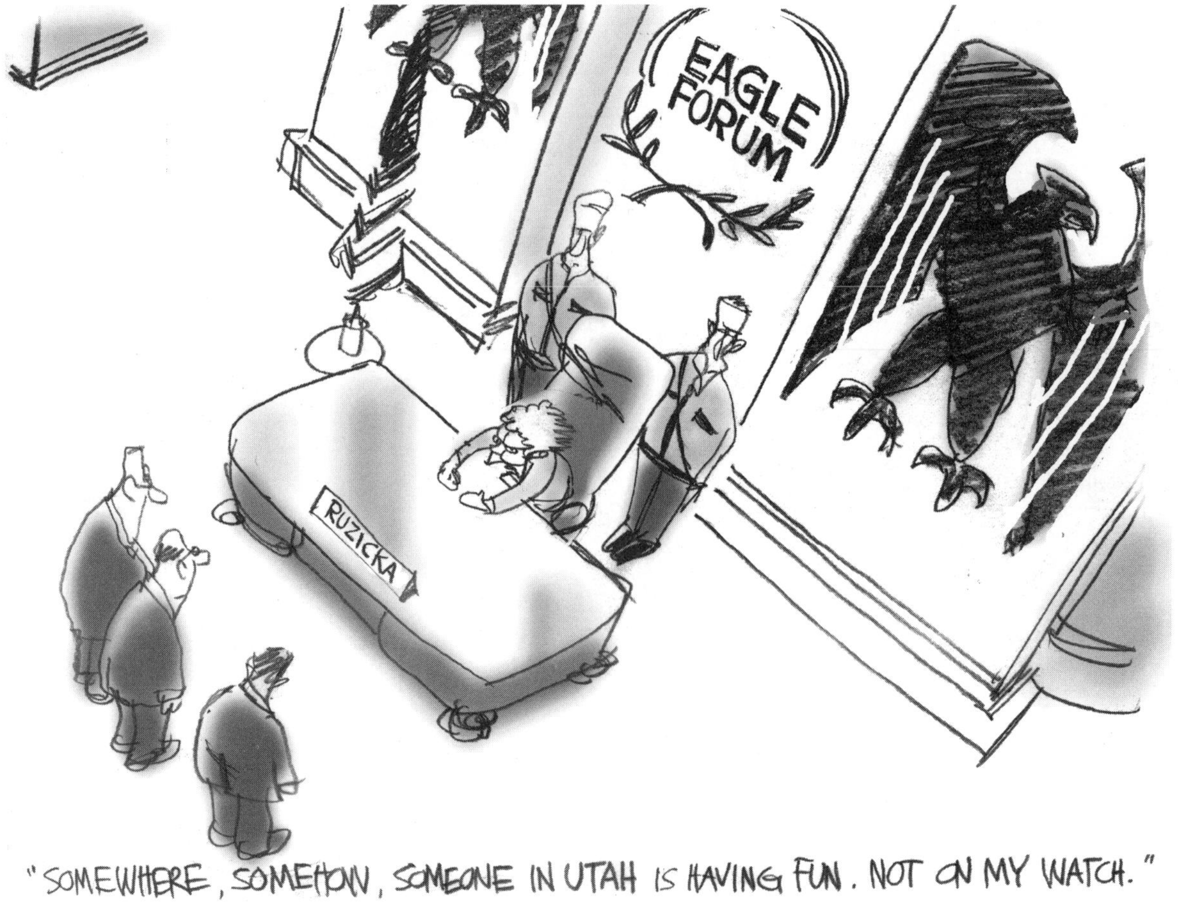
EAGLE FORUM
RUZICKA
"SOMEWHERE, SOMEHOW, SOMEONE IN UTAH IS HAVING FUN. NOT ON MY WATCH."

Gayle Ruzicka—Utah's answer to The Church Lady, only more righteous.

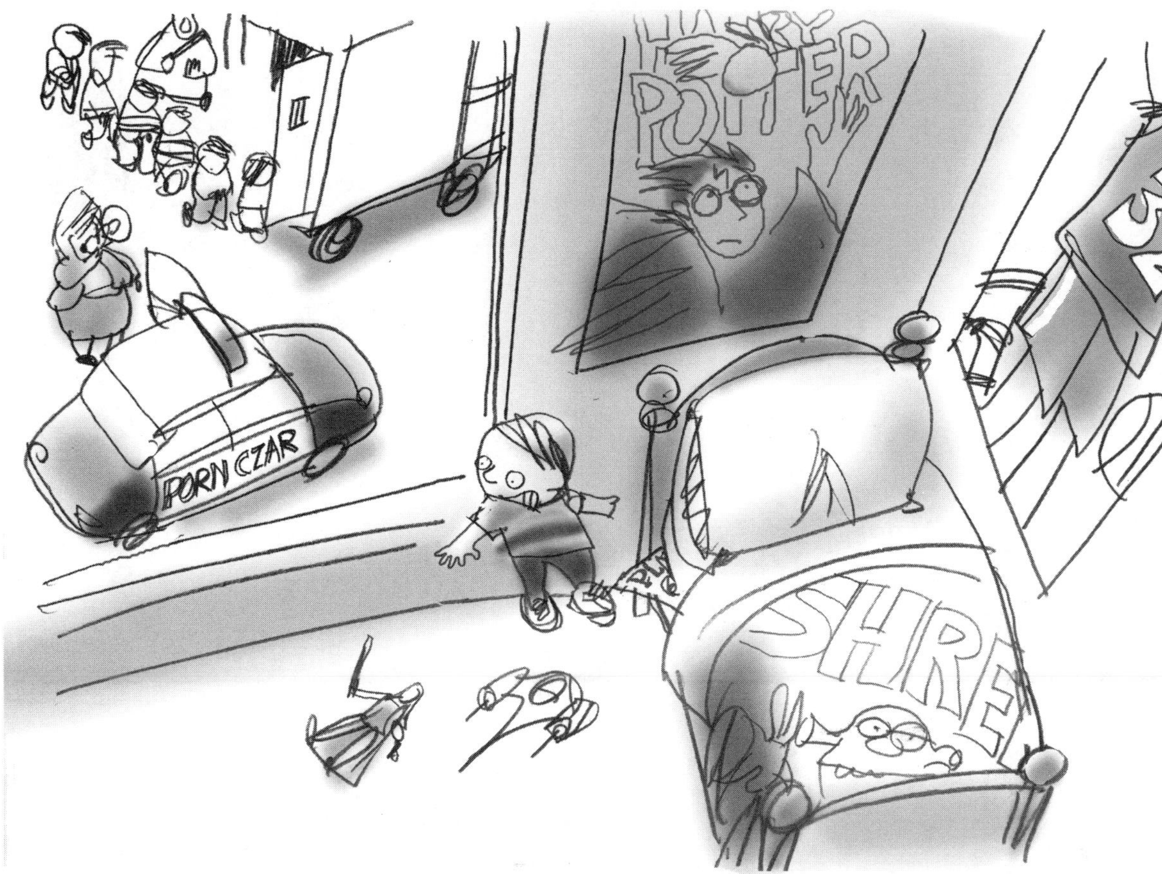
POTTER
PORN CZAR
SHRE

"WE KNOW IT'S UNDER YOUR MATTRESS, BOBBY. THROW OUT YOUR PLAYBOY AND COME OUT!"

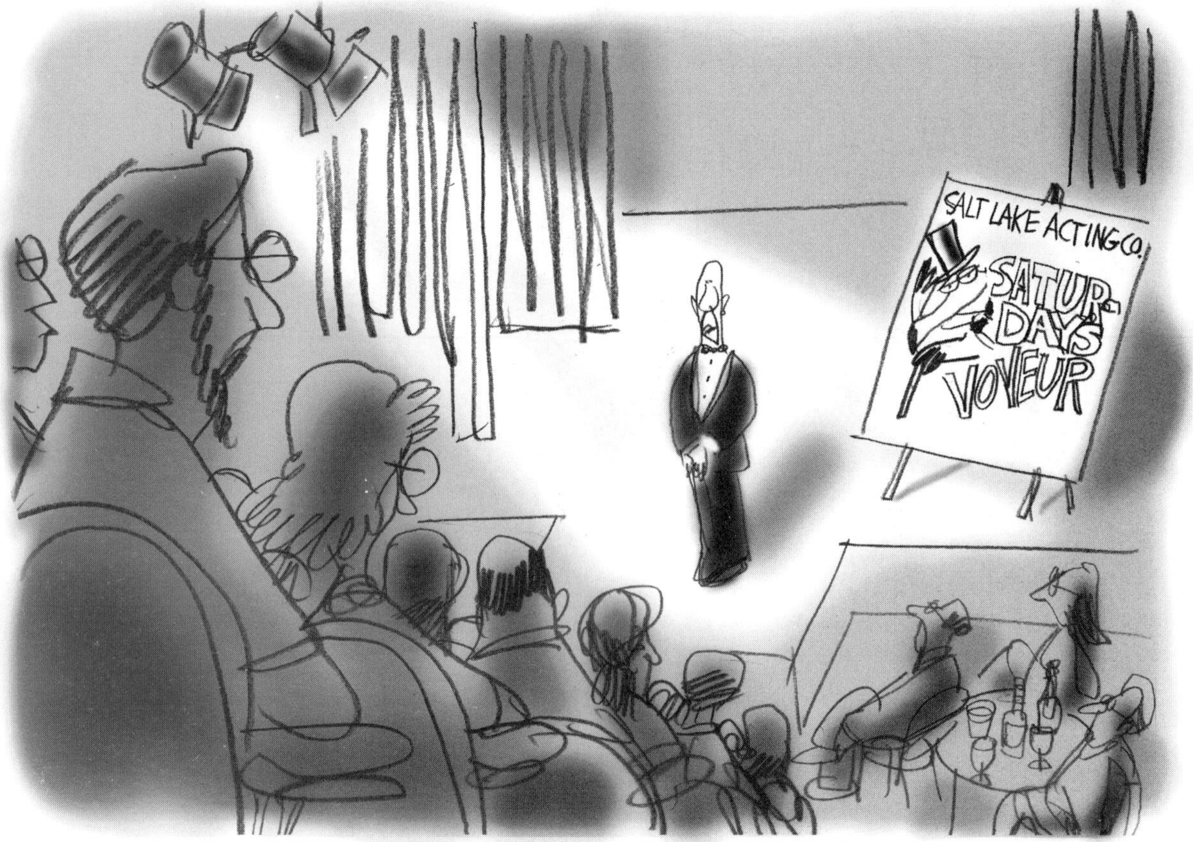
SALT LAKE ACTING CO.
SATUR-DAYS VOYEUR

"WE APOLOGIZE IF THE SATIRE SEEMS FAMILIAR-THE LEGISLATURE STOLE OUR BEST LINES."

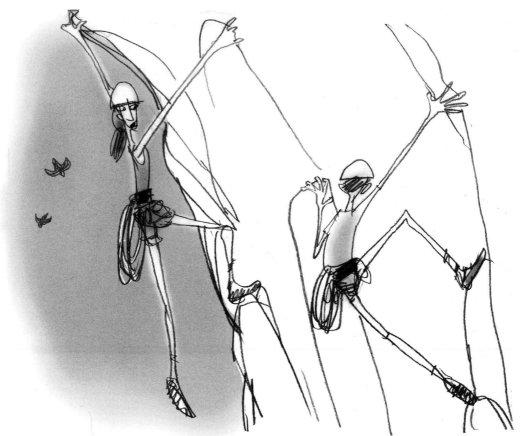

"YOU'RE TAKING THAT JOB IN MAYOR ROCKY'S OFFICE — ISN'T THAT RISKY?"

Members of Mayor Rocky Anderson's administration have a short shelf life.

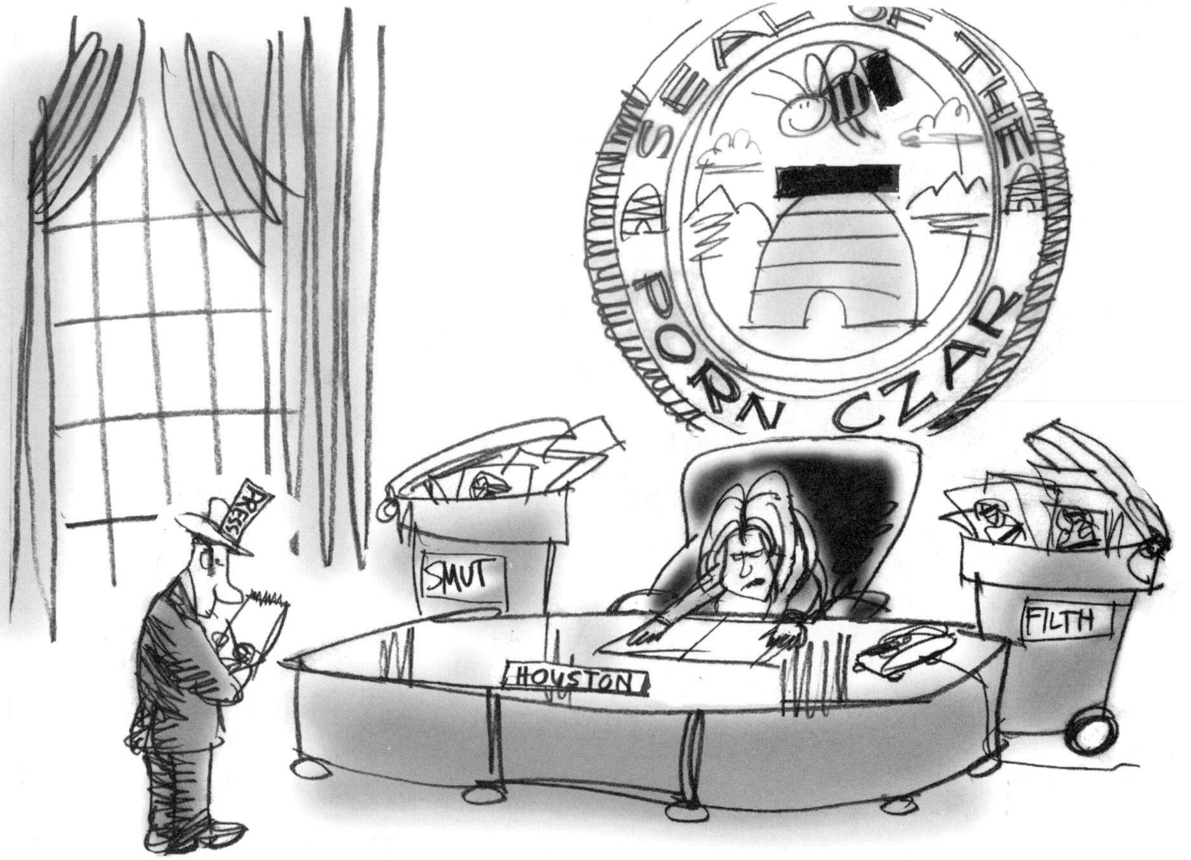
SEAL OF THE
PORN CZAR
PRESS
SMUT
FILTH
HOUSTON

"I'VE NEVER DONE ANYTHING <u>REVOLTING</u> LIKE 'HAVE SEX.' WHY IS THAT RELEVANT?"

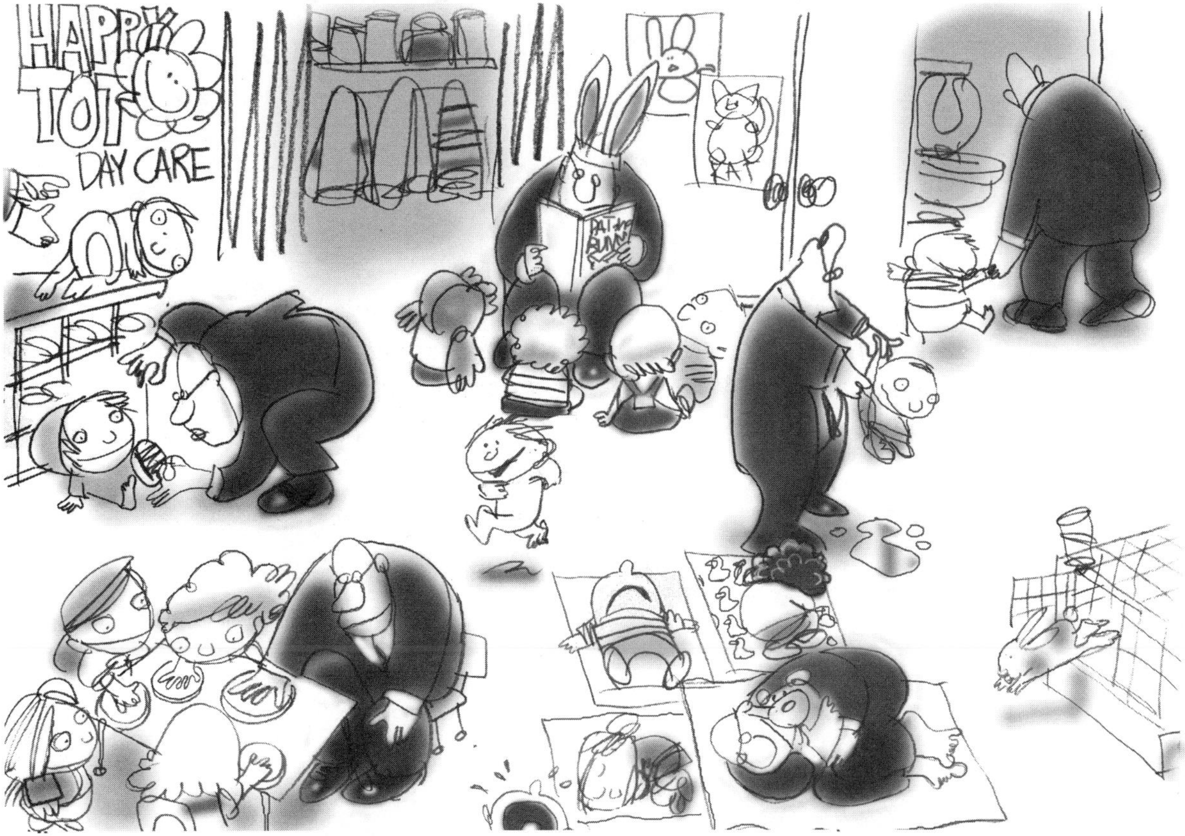
HAPPY TOT DAY CARE
PAT the BUNNY
KAT

AFTER ONLY ONE DAY ON THE JOB, UTAH LEGISLATORS AGREE TO RAISE THE MINIMUM WAGE FOR CHILD CARE PERSONNEL TO A THOUSAND BUCKS AN HOUR.

And it seemed real...in a land not too far away.
Where all the parents are strong, and wise,
and capable. Where the children are happy
and beloved. I don't know. Maybe it was Utah.

—H.I.McDonnough (Nicolas Cage)
in "Raising Arizona"

Cultural *Utah*

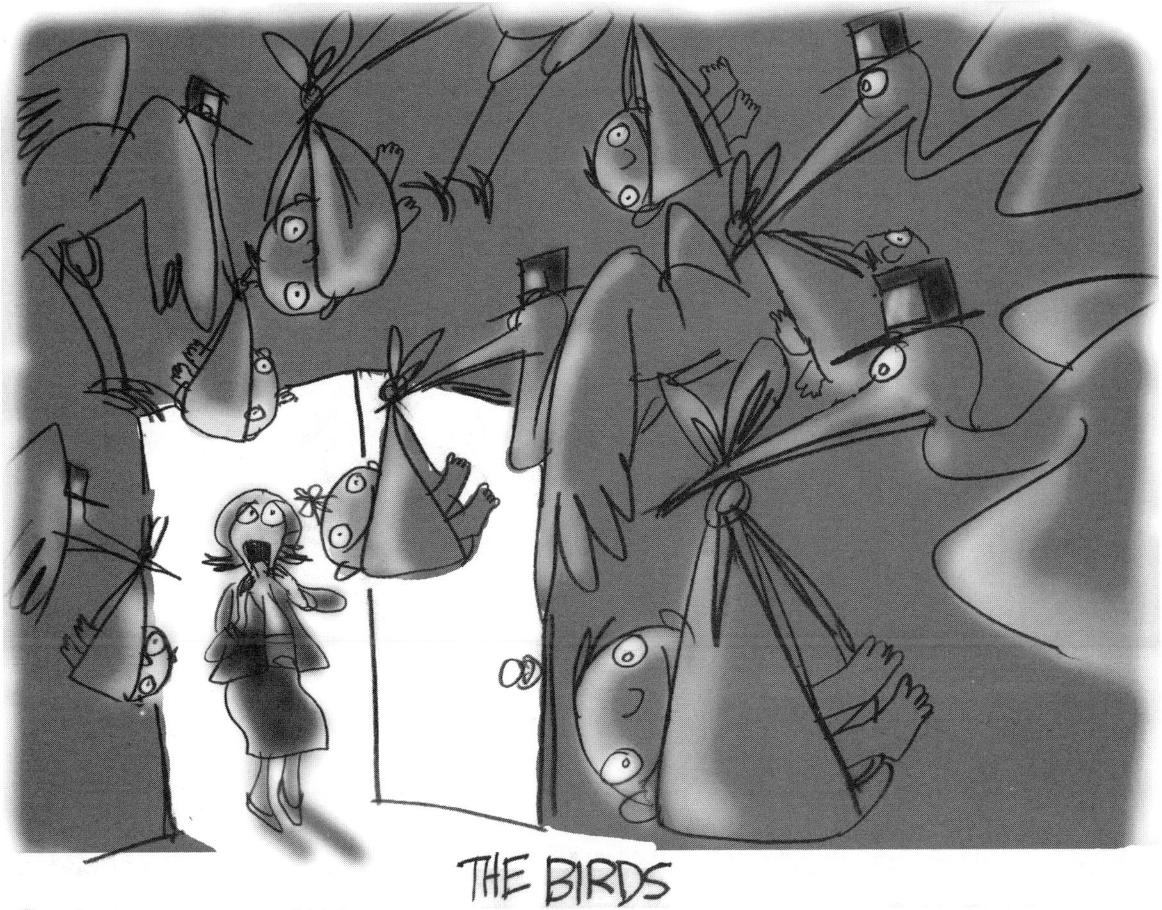
THE BIRDS

Utah remake of the Hitchcock classic.

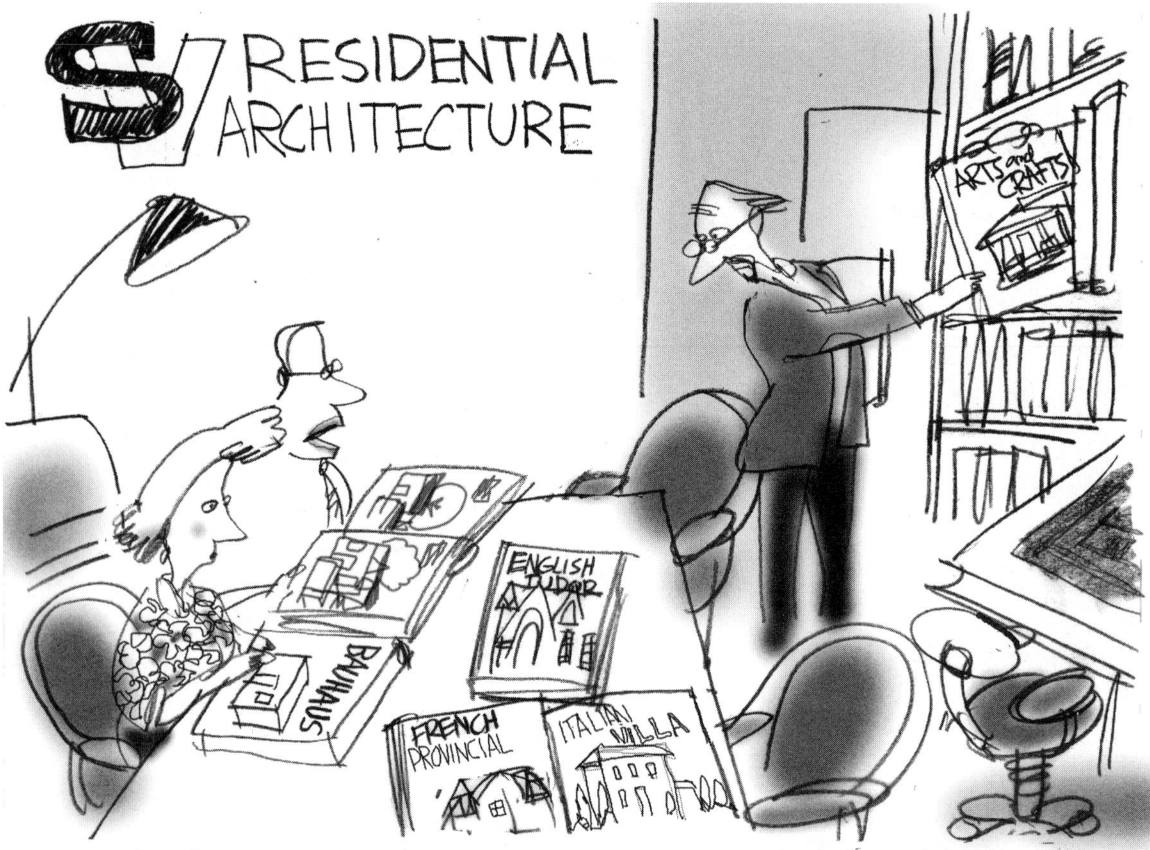
RESIDENTIAL ARCHITECTURE
ARTS and CRAFTS
ENGLISH TUDOR
BAUHAUS
FRENCH PROVINCIAL
ITALIAN VILLA

"ACTUALLY, WE'RE LOOKING FOR SOMETHING A LITTLE MORE CHURCH CONFERENCE CENTER-ISH."

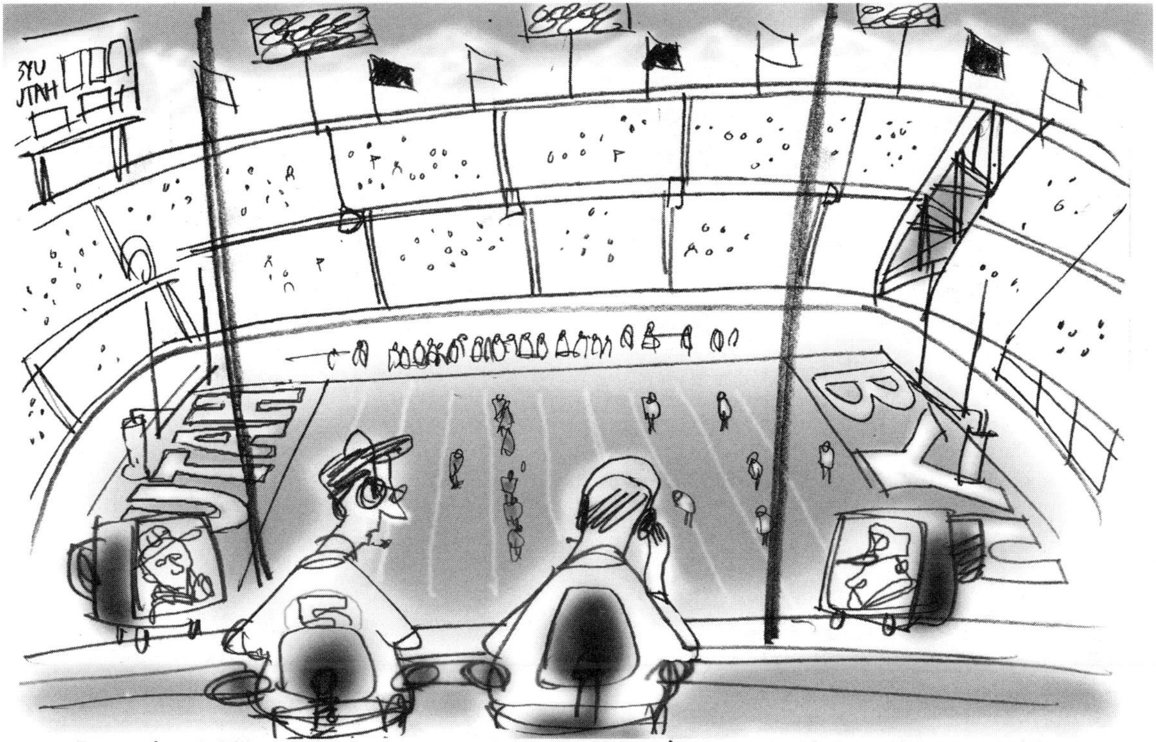

"THAT'S RIGHT, BOB, THIS IS MORE THAN A GAME TO MANY OF THESE FANS — A LOT OF TESTIMONIES COULD BE RIDING ON THE OUTCOME HERE TODAY..."

"THAT'S RIGHT, BOB — THE TRIBES OF ISRAEL AFTER HAVING SMITTEN THE HOSTS OF THE MIDIANITES COULDN'T HAVE BEEN MORE PUMPED THAN THESE COUGARS!"

Take your pick. I came up with two captions and was persuaded to leave them both.

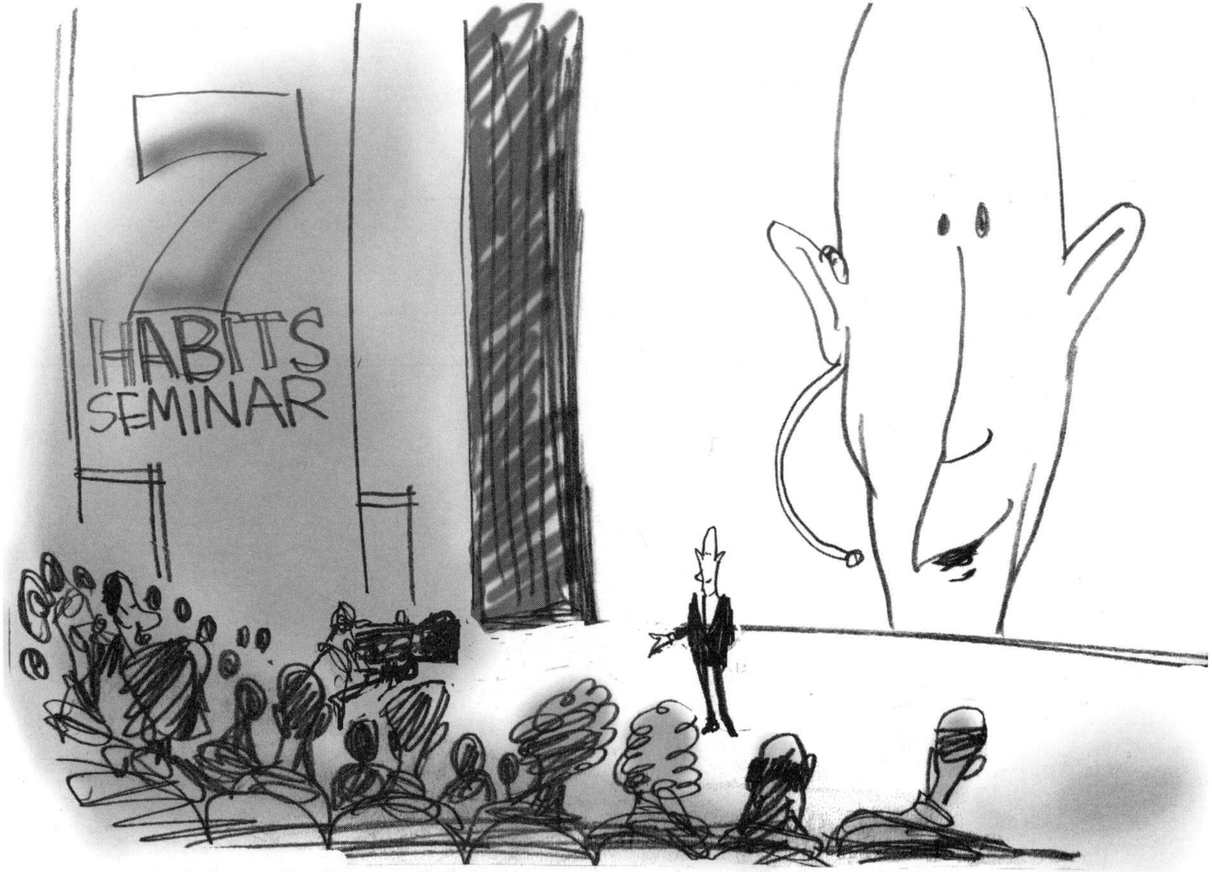
7
HABITS
SEMINAR

"WE'LL START WITH THE SEVEN HABITS OF HIGHLY SUCCESSFUL EIGHT-COW WIVES"

Local boy Stephen R. Covey is a national phenomenon.

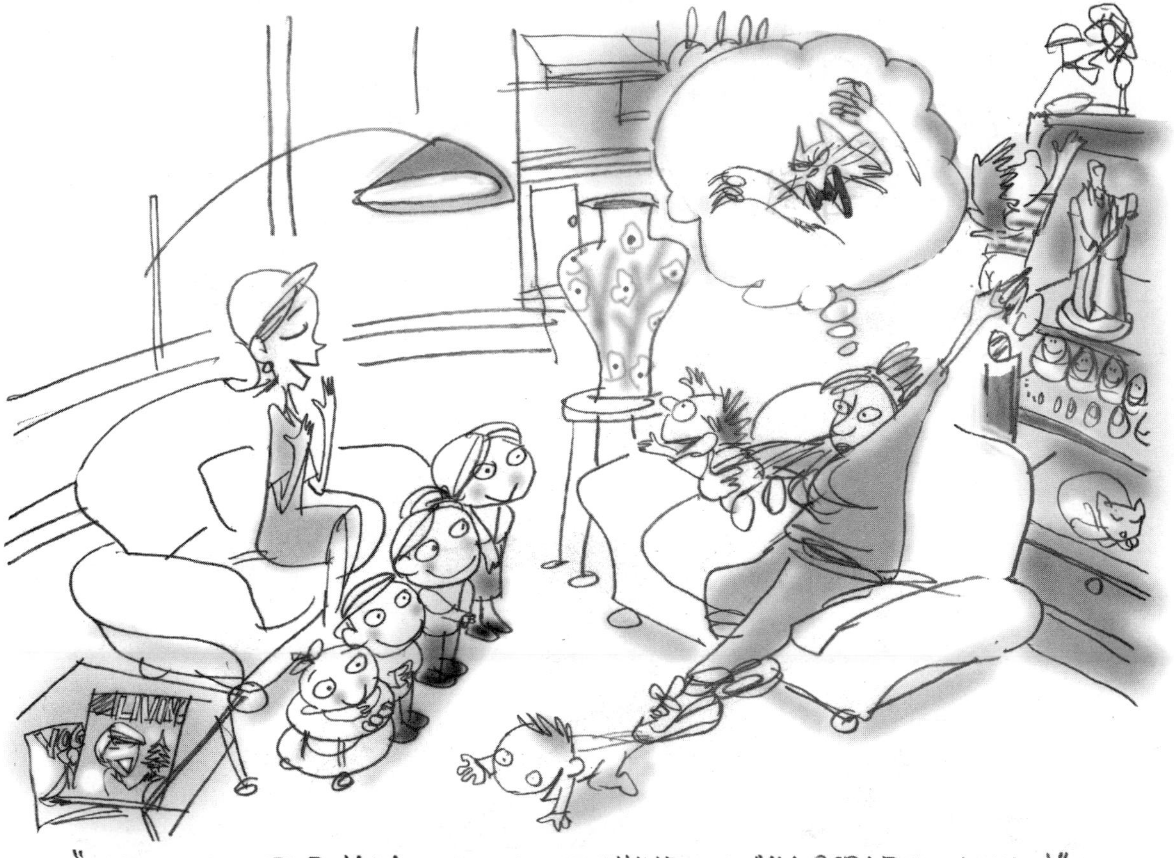

"I AM SUCH A BAD MOM – I'M DAYS BEHIND ON MY SCRAPBOOKING!"

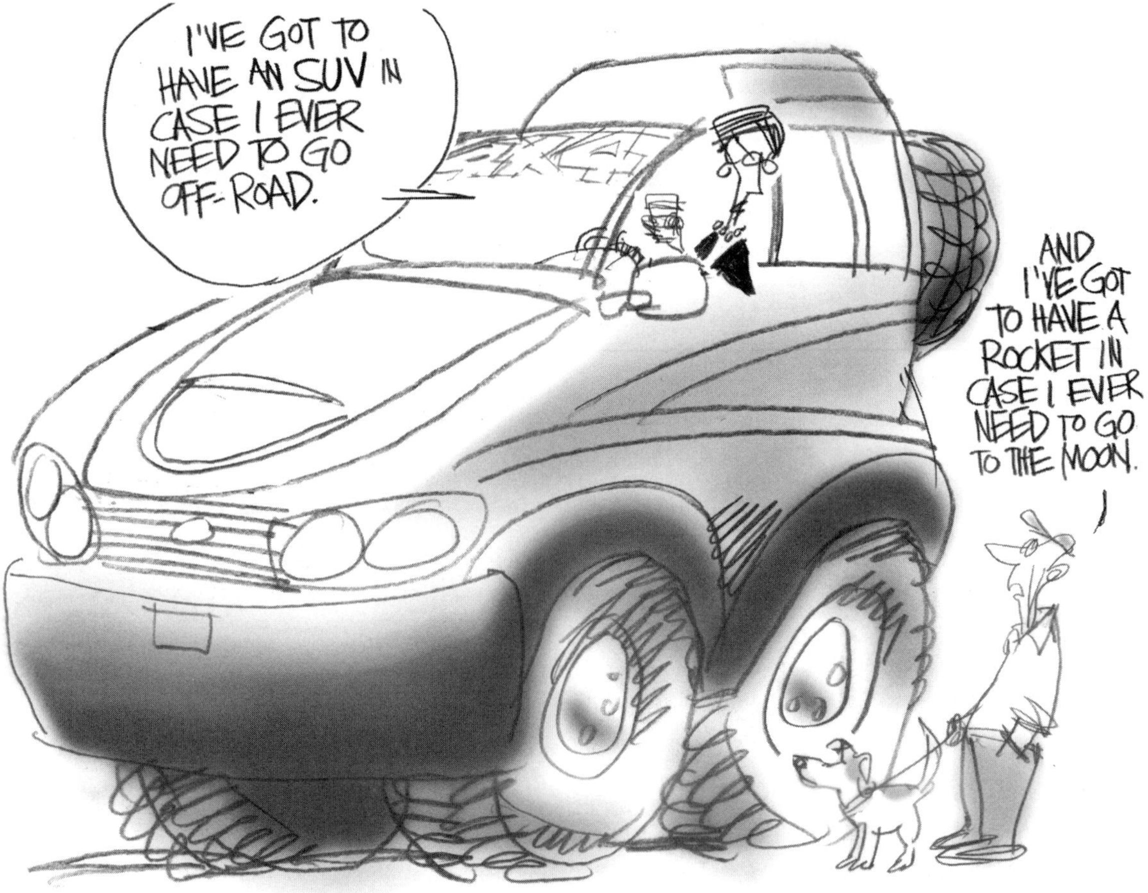
I'VE GOT TO HAVE AN SUV IN CASE I EVER NEED TO GO OFF-ROAD.
AND I'VE GOT TO HAVE A ROCKET IN CASE I EVER NEED TO GO TO THE MOON.

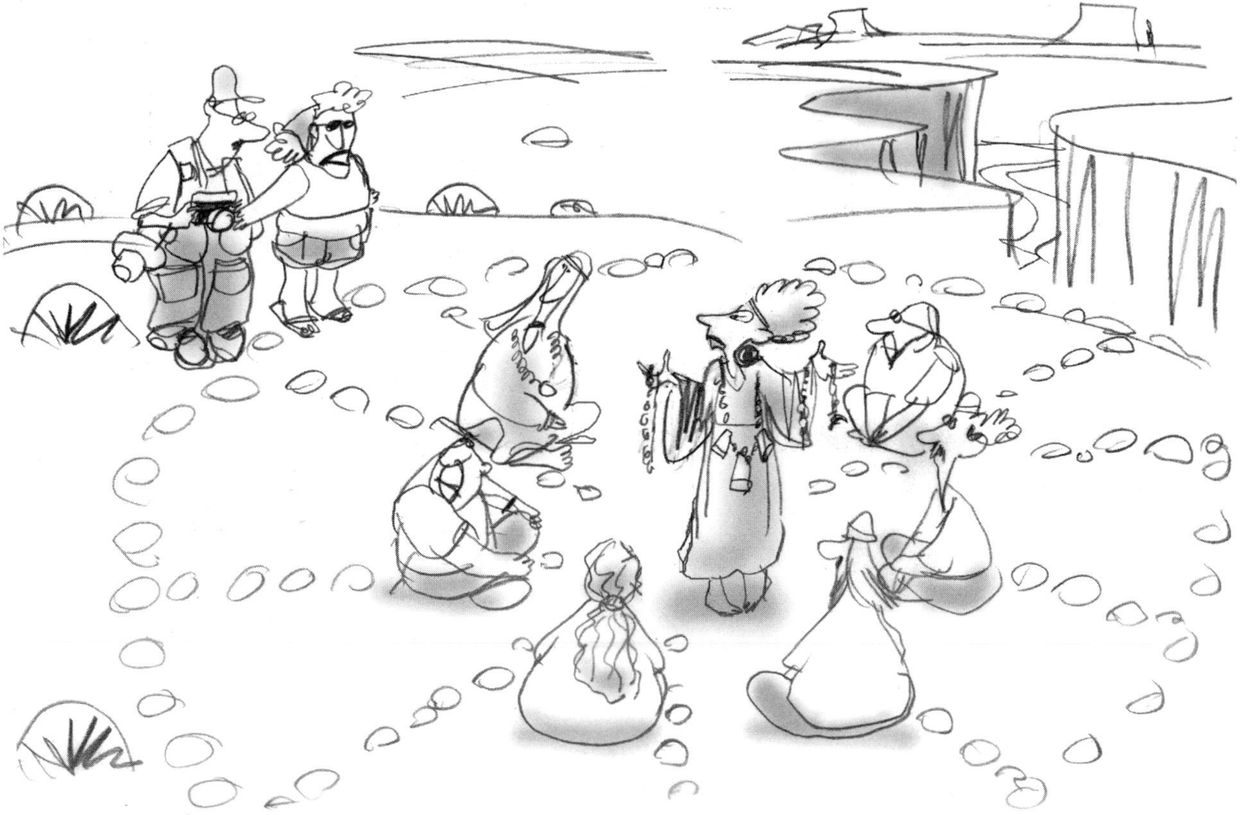

"DON'T, FRANK—THERE'S PROBABLY SOME TERRIBLE TABOO ASSOCIATED WITH TAKING PICTURES OF A FAKE INDIAN CEREMONY."

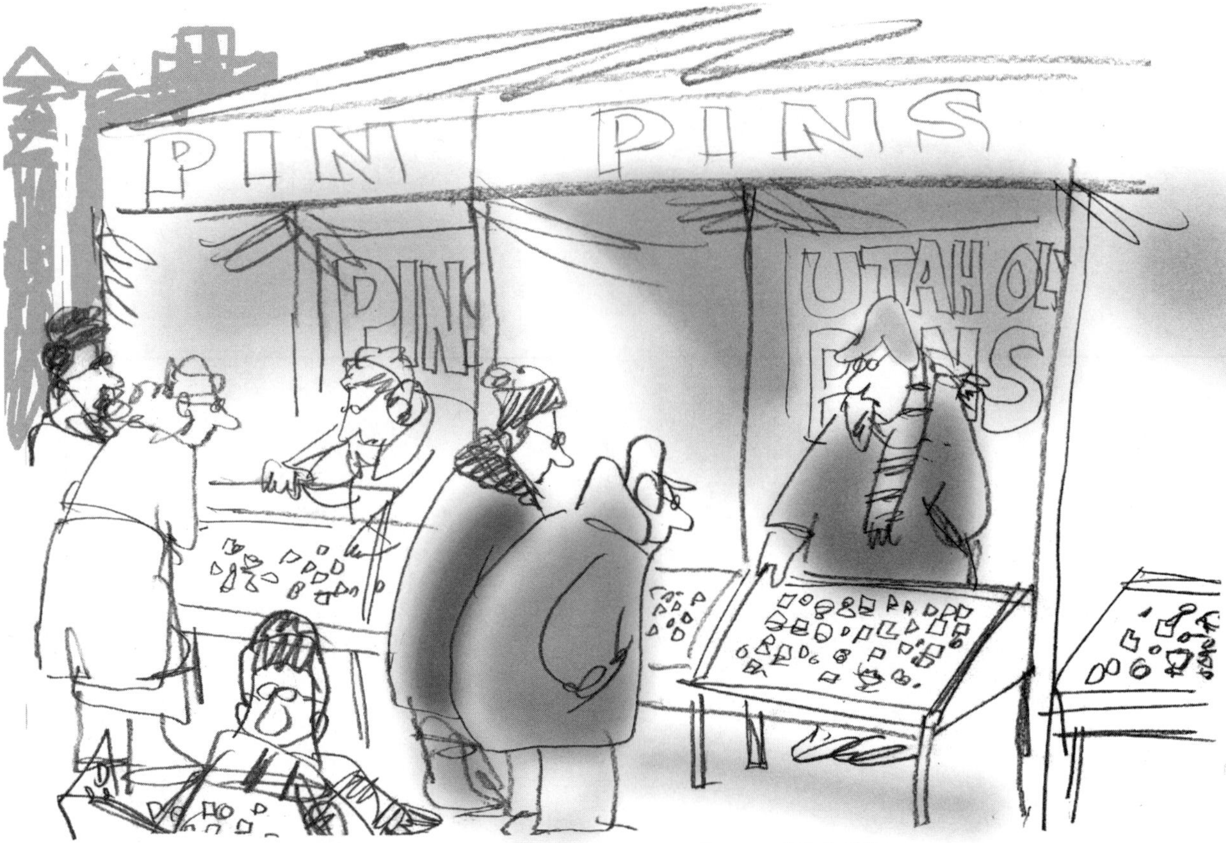
PIN PINS

"GREEN JELL-O IS THE MOST POPULAR, BUT I CAN GIVE YOU A DEAL ON THE 'COLD FUSION' OR 'POLYGAMY PRIDE' PINS."

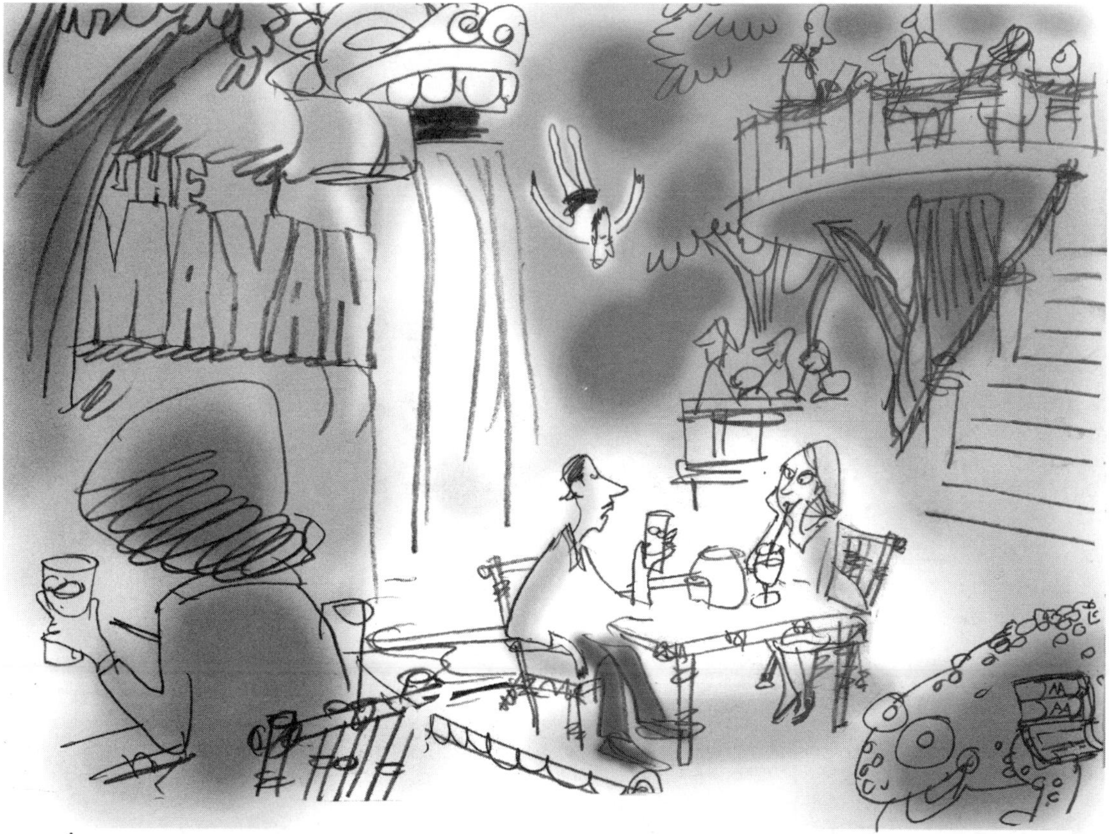
THE MAYAN

"FROM THIS LITTLE BIT OF MEXICO I WILL WHISK YOU TO A LITTLE BIT OF PARIS THAT'S JUST TWENTY MINUTES DOWN THE ROAD."

See the world without ever leaving the valley.

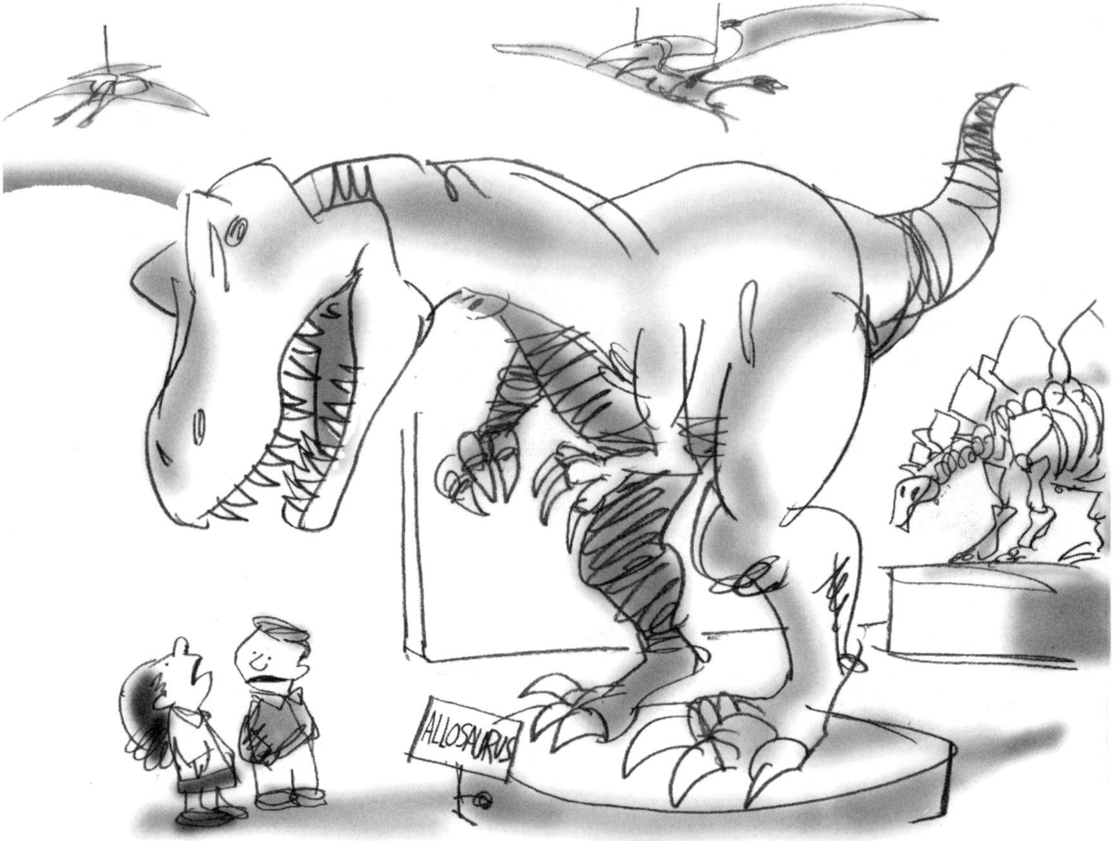
ALLOSAURUS

"MY DAD GETS THAT WAY SOMETIMES."

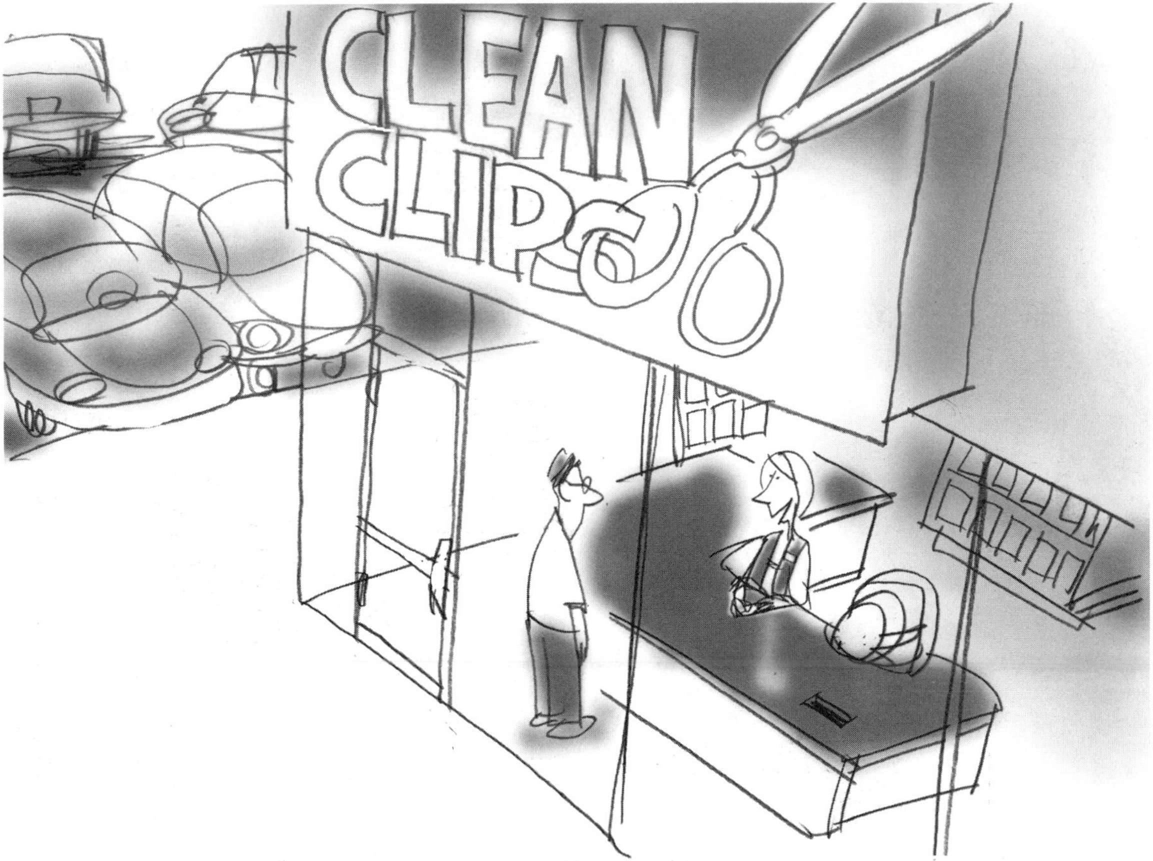
CLEAN
CLIPS

"OH, NO-WE DON'T DO HAIRCUTS-WE'RE A UTAH VALLEY VIDEO STORE."

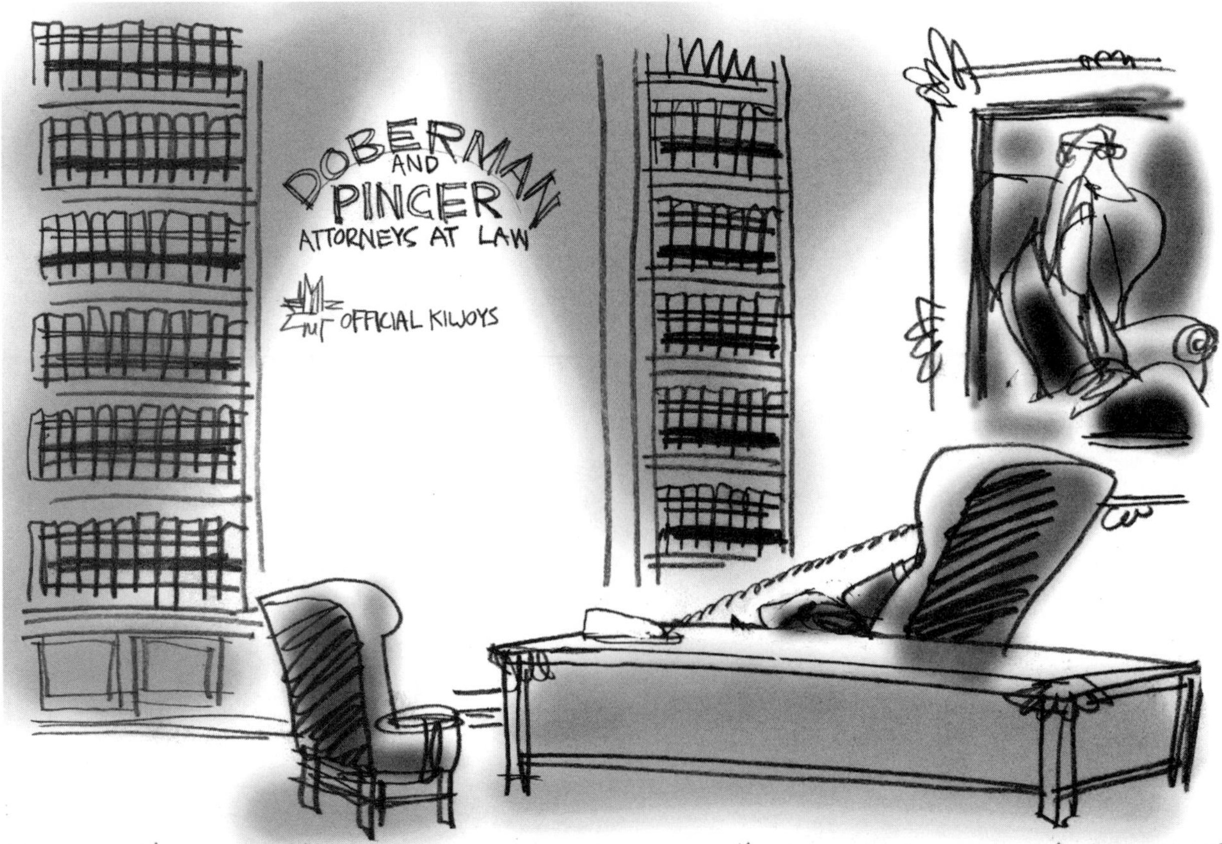
DOBERMAN AND PINCER
ATTORNEYS AT LAW
OFFICIAL KILJOYS

"'OLYMPIC', 'OLYMPICS', 'OLYMPIAD', 'OLYMPIANS' 'OLYMPIST', 'OLYMPISH', 'OLYMPICK' 'OLYMPARIAN', 'OLYMPS', 'OLYMPICNIK', 'OLYMPAROO', 'OLY', 'OLYMPICARIAN' ARE ALL COPYRIGHTED. WE'RE NOT PLAYING GAMES HERE – BY THE WAY, THAT'S COPYRIGHTED TOO."

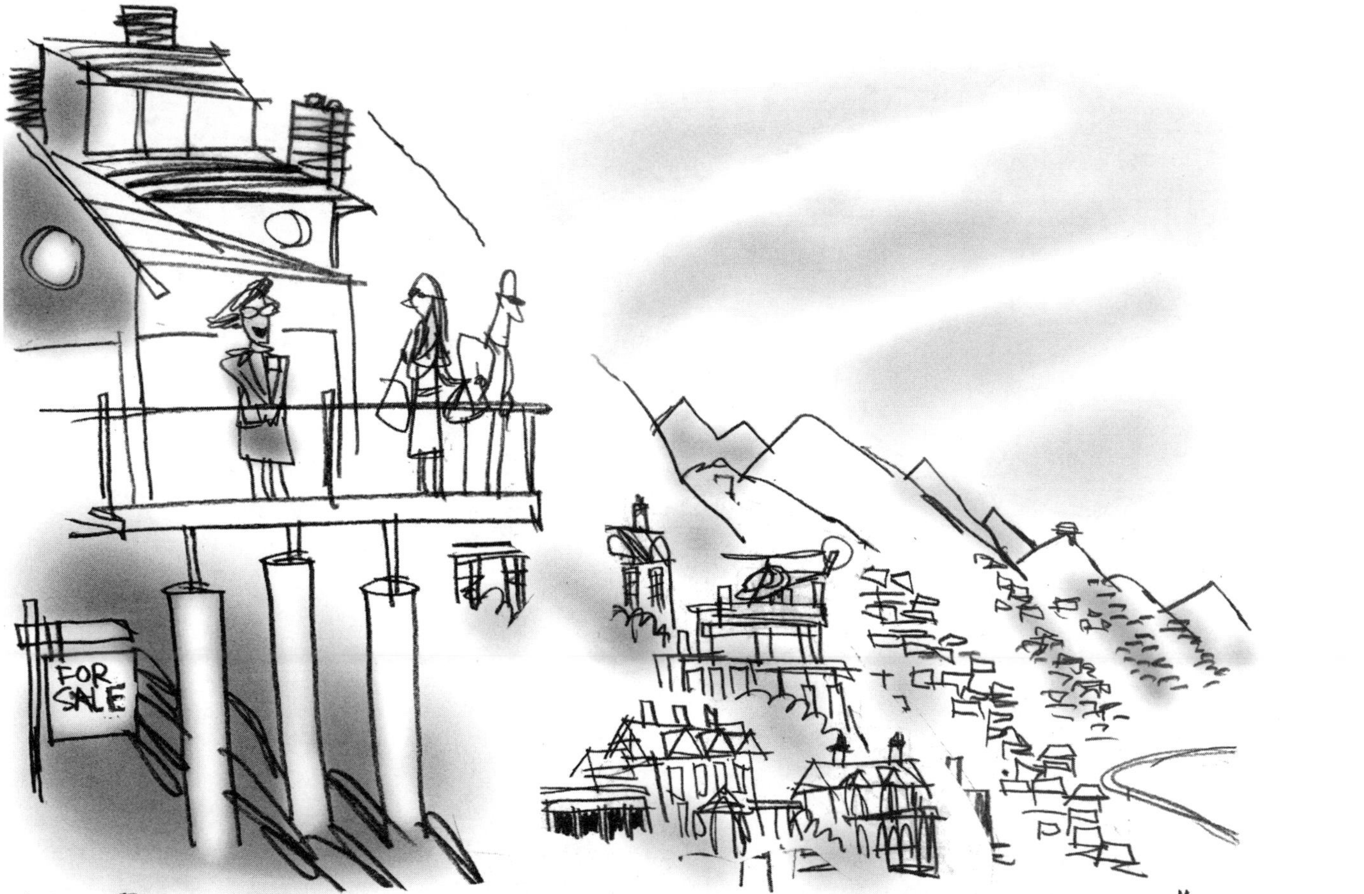
FOR SALE

"...AND FROM UP HERE YOU HAVE A MAGNIFICENT VIEW OF ALL THE LITTLE PEOPLE."

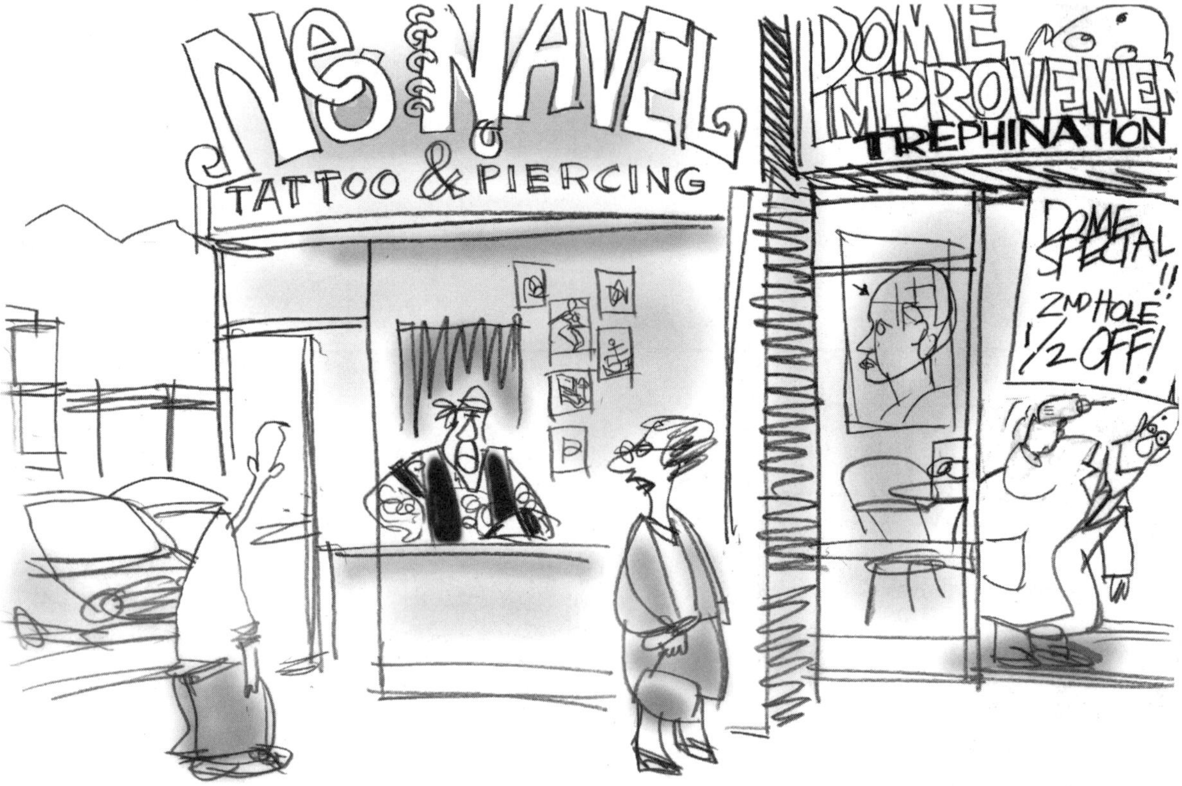
NAVEL
TATTOO & PIERCING
DOME IMPROVEMEN
TREPHINATION
DOME SPECIAL !!
2ND HOLE 1/2 OFF!

"YOU NEED THAT LIKE YOU NEED A HOLE IN THE HEAD."

A local group touts the benefits of drilling a hole through one's skull. Really.

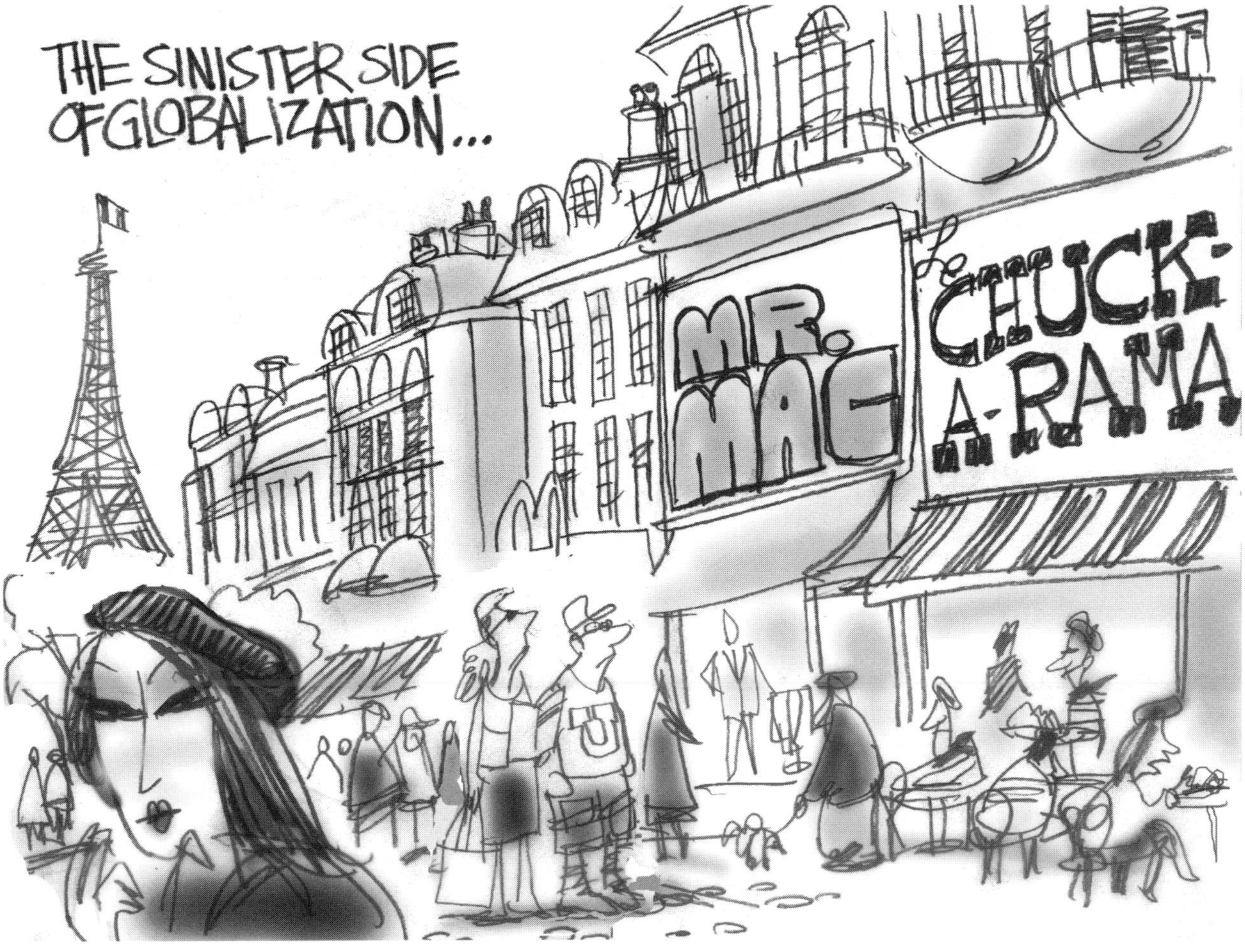

THE SINISTER SIDE OF GLOBALIZATION...
MR. MAC
Le CHUCK-A-RAMA

The
End

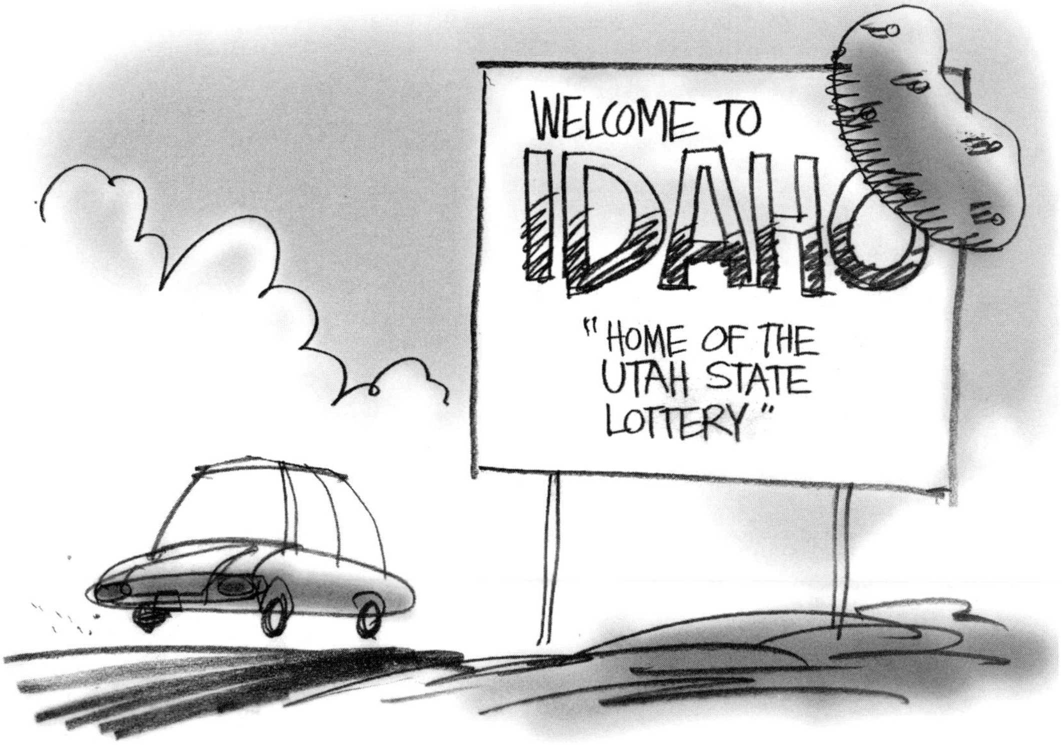
WELCOME TO
IDAHO
"HOME OF THE
UTAH STATE
LOTTERY"